Personal Records

Personal Records

A GALLERY OF
SELF-PORTRAITS

Selected by

MARGARET BOTTRALL

THE JOHN DAY COMPANY
New York

First American Edition 1962

© 1961 by Margaret Bottrall

Published by The John Day Company,
62 West 45 Street, New York, 36, N.Y.

Library of Congress Catalog Card
Number: 62–15132

PRINTED IN GREAT BRITAIN BY
HAZELL WATSON AND VINEY LTD
AYLESBURY AND SLOUGH

22847

Contents

INTRODUCTION 7

EARLY YEARS 13

EXPANDING HORIZONS 47

SELF-SCRUTINISERS 75

WOMEN IN LOVE 107

PASTIME AND GOOD
  COMPANY 129

AFFLICTED AND DISTRESSED 163

DEDICATED SPIRITS 193

BIOGRAPHICAL INDEX 215

Acknowledgements

I am indebted to the following publishers and copyright holders for permission to use extracts from copyright works:

Messrs. George Allen & Unwin for Augustus Hare's *The Years with Mother*, edited by Malcolm Barnes.

The Bodley Head for *Squire Osbaldeston: His Autobiography*, edited by E. D. Cuming.

Messrs. Jonathan Cape Ltd. for Eric Gill's *Autobiography*.

Mrs H. M. Davies and Messrs. Jonathan Cape Ltd. for W. H. Davies, *Autobiography of a Super-tramp*.

Messrs. Chatto & Windus Ltd. for W. N. P. Barbellion's *The Journal of a Disappointed Man*.

The Clarendon Press for R. G. Collingwood's *Autobiography*.

Messrs. J. M. Dent & Sons Ltd. for Joseph Conrad's *A Personal Record*.

Messrs. William Heinemann Ltd. for Edmund Gosse's *Father and Son*.

David Higham Associates Ltd. for *The Denton Welch Journals*, edited by Jocelyn Brooke, published by Hamish Hamilton.

The Hogarth Press for Edwin Muir's *Autobiography* and for Sir Leslie Stephen's *Some Early Impressions*.

The Hutchinson Publishing Group for G. K. Chesterton's *Autobiography* (1936) and for *Memoirs of William Hickey*, edited by Arthur Spence (1913).

Mr C. D. Medley for George Moore's *Confessions of a Young Man*, published by Heinemann.

Messrs. Methuen & Co. Ltd. for Dudley Ryder's *Autobiography*.

The Passfield Trust for Beatrice Wbb's *My Apprenticeship*, published by Messrs. Longmans, Green & Co.

The Royal Society for the Protection of Birds, and the Society of Authors for W. H. Hudson's *Far Away and Long Ago*, published by Dent.

The executors of H. G. Wells and Messrs. A. P. Watt & Son for H. G. Wells' *Experiment in Autobiography*, published by Gollancz.

Mrs W. B. Yeats, Messrs. A. P. Watt & Son, and Messrs. Macmillan & Co. for W. B. Yeats' *Autobiographies*.

Introduction

ON the walls of a picture-gallery, self-portraits are quickly identifiable, even when we know nothing of the painters concerned. Sometimes the raised palette or the poised brush is obvious evidence; but always unmistakable are the scrutinising eyes, the expression of concentrated attention as the artist gazes into the unseen mirror. What is he looking for? Not the physical features only, though these are of paramount importance. He seeks also those personal qualities, most characteristic of himself, which he wants to convey through brush-strokes on the canvas. Occasionally, as though dissatisfied by the commonplace image reflected in the glass, he resorts to some kind of fancy dress—a turban, a plumed hat. Mere accuracy is not what he aims at, but rather the portrayal of his individuality. A self-portraitist needs psychological insight as well as technical virtuosity, and this is true whether he works in the medium of colours or in words.

The tasks of painter and writer are not, however, entirely similar, for the painter is concerned with the present moment; the writer is equally concerned with all that has led up to the present. One might argue that the human countenance, at any instant, is what its past has made it, but a painter cannot indicate the stages by which a brow grows furrowed or a mouth takes on a petulant droop; he can only record how the subject appeared, in that particular light, on that particular day.

The autobiographer may sometimes be animated by the same desire as impels the artist to delineate his present self; but even if he is particularly interested in examining the personality he actually is, chronology nearly always enters into his method. Not all autobiographers, by any means, are introspective enough to ask "What do I amount to as a man?" but almost all try to indicate how they have come to be what they are. The forces that truly shape a human personality are not always obvious, and the individual concerned is likely to be blinder to the significance of formative events than those who can observe from a detached viewpoint; so, more often than not, the autobiographer takes the line of least resistance. He begins with a brief account of his origins and upbringing, and then proceeds chronologically, selecting and dwelling on those episodes which, in retrospect, appear important and interesting.

There are therefore very strong arguments against making an anthology of autobiographical extracts, for the better an auto- biography is, the more it demands to be read in its entirety. Skilful writers present us with their developing selves; modi- fications of beliefs, changes of heart, these common phenomena are only to be understood in the context of the whole life in which they occur.

What justification, then, can there be for snipping extracts from books which rely for their full effect on continuity and accumulation of detail? Only I think, the pleasure that can be derived from meeting a heterogeneous company of men and women, all articulate and eager to talk about themselves—a pleasure analogous to that of strolling round a gallery full of self-portraits, in so far as it may quicken our appreciation of the variety of human types who share a passion for regarding them- selves in the mirrors of memory or self-scrutiny.

In this gallery of autobiographers, however, it will be observed that many of the pictures are more like conversation-pieces than self-portraits. Several figures are in evidence; they converse, gesticulate, take action. One reason for the inclusion of these pieces is that a collection confined to introspective self-analyses would be monotonous and productive of boredom. Another is that the majority of human beings reveal themselves best in social and even in dramatic situations. Their behaviour is a far better indication of their temperament and beliefs than any remarks which they are capable of making about themselves. So here we have narratives and episodes that display, obliquely and sometimes unintentionally, the characters of their authors, as well as passages of self-scrutiny and conscious assessment.

It has not, however, seemed relevant to include extracts from memoirs which derive their main interest from reminiscences about the writer's contemporaries. There are vast numbers of such books, many of them fascinating, especially to the social or literary historian. But glorified scandal and gossip, like the memoirs of Harriette Wilson or Letitia Pilkington, come closer to biography (if not to fiction) than to autobiography; and even such an indefatigable and earnest chronicler as Crabb Robinson does not begin to qualify as a self-portraitist.

For a similar reason, there are few extracts from those life-histories, often very readable and entertaining, in which the personality of the writer is wholly subordinate to the adventures that befall him. Such tales belong to the category of true-adventure-story rather than to autobiographer proper. It is true that some of the people depicted in this book led exciting lives, which they recounted at length. William Cobbett in America, Silas Told on the slave-trading ships or preaching to the condemned at Newgate and Tyburn, Thomas Holcroft in his progress from stable-boy to radical politician—these, and many others here represented, were men of action; but they did take more than an intermittent interest in their own personal identities and in the qualities that distinguished them as individuals. It is this that marks them off from the memoir-writer who is merely the central character of an adventurous narrative or traveller's tale.

It would have been possible to diversify the contents of this gallery by including some landscapes or carefully studied interiors, since there are some autobiographers who have chosen to reconstruct their past, and specially their childhood, more by an evocation of places and things than by personal reminiscence. Percy Lubbock's *Earlham* and George Bourne's *The Wheelwright's Shop* in their different ways exemplify this method. But the emphasis in this book is not on environment or social change; rather, it is on human idiosyncrasy.

Consequently the extracts have been arranged in the hope of producing a certain pleasure from juxtapositions which may be unexpected. Though the relation between one passage and its neighbour may sometimes be tenuous, the idea has been either to bring out the similarities which exist in spite of differences in period or circumstance, or by sharp contrast to provide reminders of the fascinating varieties in the English character. Certain pieces seemed to gravitate towards one another; others had to be tried first in one position, then in another, because they contained affinities with several different passages. To anyone arranging an exhibition, how to hang the pictures is a thorny and almost insoluble problem, for even when decisions have been taken, attractive alternatives present themselves. My categories, if somewhat arbitrary, at least impose a certain coherence on what would otherwise be a mere miscellany.

The first two are self-explanatory—*Early Years* and *Expanding Horizons*. More often than not, the most entertaining chapters of an autobiography are those which deal with childhood and upbringing. Even quite tedious chroniclers are capable of good writing here; the long perspective, the sense of comparative detachment and the abiding vividness of early recollections seem to fire their pens. Thomas Holcroft, who died in 1809, was exceptional in his times in writing a full account of the first fifteen years of his life, and explicitly declaring the importance he attached to the recording of childish experience. On the whole, autobiographical studies of childhood belong to the twentieth century; Edmund Gosse, with his *Father and Son* (1907), was a pioneer in the genre. Most of those of outstanding merit have been written by people in whom the creative imagination remains strong, poets or artists. For such people, the years of their childhood are often the most significant of all. Senses and intelligence have not yet been dulled by convention, but respond to the mystery of existence. The ancestor of those who write nostalgically and sensitively about their childhood is Thomas Traherne, to whom priority of place has been given in the first section. But for one poet or artist who may share Traherne's sense of an age of innocence, there are dozens of ordinary people who look back on their childhood with an affectionate, sometimes humorous detachment. Such people write well and freely, too, about their schooldays, apprenticeships or undergraduate years. These stages of life are all represented in the section *Expanding Horizons.*

The third section is devoted to examples of deliberate self-analysis. Some are brief extracts from journals which nobody but the writer was expected to read; some come from chapters written in old age, like the passages by Darwin and Wells, in which the whole mental and spiritual constitution is subjected to review.

The fourth, *Women in Love,* needs no explanation, unless a word is needed about Harriet Martineau, a woman certainly not in love at the time when she wrote the excerpt. But she speaks so pertinently about the place of love in an average woman's life, and so courageously about the satisfactions of work, that she seems to set off the others to advantage.

In the fifth section there is only one character who is not notably good-humoured, Adam Martindale; but one spoilsport throws into relief the general jollity of the others. In actual life, not all of them were sociable; Edward Lear, for one, was not; but in these passages at least they are inclined to assert that life is thoroughly worth living. Contrasting with this section, the sixth comprises extracts from writers peculiarly sensitive to suffering. In the final section, we find a group drawn together by a common regard for what Blake calls "the Dictates of our Angels"—poets, artists and religious converts, all dedicated spirits.

Poems, letters and journals have been drawn on, as well as formal autobiographies, for the sake of variety and amusement, but there are no passages from living writers. This is not for lack of material but rather because of its enormous bulk. The output of memoirs and personal records over the last fifty years has been stupendous. Diplomats, society hostesses, taxi-drivers, field-marshals, journalists, travellers, prostitutes, tycoons, all seem to have leisure, sooner or later, to put pen to paper and transcribe such portions of their life-histories as they deem memorable and marketable. But besides these ephemeral productions, there have been a great many extremely interesting and distinguished autobiographies written during the twentieth century. It seems, indeed, likely enough that literary assessors a hundred years hence may rate our narratives of fact higher than our fiction. The best autobiographies of recent years are not difficult to obtain, and it is better to read them whole than to sample them. There are in this gallery, however, a few near-contemporary studies, to indicate that the art of self-portraiture is in a flourishing state. They are there, too, to demonstrate the continuity of human types and human problems. Literary conventions change, but whether the writers here represented use the current idiom or archaic phrases, they can usually elicit from us a smile of fellow-feeling.

Early Years

THOMAS TRAHERNE

W. H. HUDSON

SILAS TOLD

THOMAS HOLCROFT

SAMUEL JOHNSON

S. T. COLERIDGE

LUCY HUTCHINSON

C. M. YONGE

MARY ROBINSON

JOHN RUSKIN

AUGUSTUS HARE

EDMUND GOSSE

R. D. OWEN

ALEXANDER SOMERVILLE

Thomas Traherne

CERTAINLY Adam in Paradise had not more sweet and curious apprehensions of the world, than I when I was a child.

All appeared new and strange at first, inexpressibly rare and delightful and beautiful. I was a little stranger, which at my entrance into the world was saluted and surrounded with innumerable joys. My knowledge was divine. I knew by intuition those things which since my apostasy I collected again by the highest reason. My very ignorance was advantageous. I seemed as one brought into the estate of innocence. All things were spotless and pure and glorious; yea, and infinitely mine, and joyful and precious. I knew not that there were any sins, or complaints or laws. I dreamed not of poverties, contentions or vices. All tears and quarrels were hidden from mine eyes. Everything was at rest, free and immortal. I knew nothing of sickness or death or rents or exaction, either for tribute or bread. In the absence of these I was entertained like an angel with the works of God in their splendour and glory, I saw all in the peace of Eden; heaven and earth did sing my Creator's praises, and could not make more melody to Adam, than to me. All time was eternity, and a perpetual Sabbath. Is it not strange, that an infant should be heir of the whole world, and see those mysteries which the books of the learned never unfold?

The corn was orient and immortal wheat, which never should be reaped, nor was ever sown. I thought it had stood from everlasting to everlasting. The dust and stones of the street were as precious as gold: the gates were at first the end of the world. The green trees when I saw them first through one of the gates transported and ravished me, their sweetness and unusual beauty made my heart to leap, and almost mad with ecstasy, they were such strange and wonderful things. The men! O what venerable and reverend creatures did the aged seem! Immortal Cherubims! And young men glittering and sparkling angels, and maids strange seraphic pieces of life and beauty! Boys and girls tumbling in the street, and playing, were moving jewels. I knew not that they were born or should die; but all things abided eternally as they were in their proper places. Eternity was manifested in the light of the day, and something infinite behind everything appeared, which talked with my expectation and moved my desire. The city seemed to stand in Eden, or to be built in Heaven. The streets were mine, the temple was mine, the people were mine, their clothes and gold and silver were mine, as much as their sparkling eyes, fair skins and ruddy faces. The skies were mine, and so were the sun and moon and stars, and all the world was mine, and I the only spectator and enjoyer of it. I knew no churlish proprieties, nor bounds, nor divisions; but all proprieties and divisions were mine: all treasures and the possessors of them. So that with much ado I was corrupted, and made to learn the dirty devices of this world. Which now I unlearn, and become as it were a little child again that I may enter into the Kingdom of God.

Centuries of Meditation.

W. H. Hudson

My memory takes me back to a time when the delight I experienced in all natural things was purely physical. I rejoiced in colours, scents, sounds, in taste and touch; the blue of the sky, the verdure of earth, the sparkle of sunlight on water, the taste of milk, of fruit, of honey, the smell of dry or moist soil, of wind and rain, of herbs and flowers; the mere feel of a blade of grass made me happy; and there were certain sounds and perfumes, and above all certain colours in flowers, and in the plumage and eggs of birds, such as the purple polished shell of the tinamou's egg, which intoxicated me with delight. When, riding on the plain, I discovered a patch of scarlet verbenas in full bloom, the creeping plants covering an area of several yards, with a moist, green sward sprinkled abundantly with the shining flower-bosses, I would throw myself from my pony with a cry of joy to lie on the turf among them and feast my sight on the brilliant colour.

It was not, I think, till my eighth year that I began to be distinctly conscious of something more than this mere childish delight in nature. It may have been there all the time from infancy—I don't know; but when I began to know it consciously it was as if some hand had surreptitiously dropped something into the honeyed cup which gave it at certain times a new flavour. It gave me little thrills, often purely pleasurable, at other times startling, and there were occasions when it became so poignant as to frighten me. The sight of a magnificent sunset was sometimes almost more than I could endure and made me wish to hide myself away. But when the feeling was roused by the sight of a small and beautiful or singular object, such as a flower, its sole effect was to intensify the object's loveliness. There were many flowers which produced this effect in but a slight degree, and as I grew up and the animistic sense lost its intensity, these too lost their magic and were almost like other flowers which had never had it. . . .

The feeling, however, was evoked more powerfully by trees than by even the most supernatural of my flowers; it varied in power according to time and place and the appearance of the tree or trees, and always affected me most on moonlight nights. Frequently, after I had first begun to experience it consciously, I would go out of my way to meet it, and I used to steal out of the house alone when the moon was at its full to stand, silent and motionless, near some group of large trees, gazing at the dusky green foliage silvered by the beams; and at such times the sense of mystery would grow until a sensation of delight would change to fear, and the fear increase until it was no longer to be borne, and I would hastily escape to recover the sense of reality and safety indoors, where there was light and company. Yet on the very next night I would steal out again and go to the spot where the effect was strongest, which was usually among the large locust or white acacia trees, which gave the name of Las Acacias to our place. The loose feathery foliage on moonlight nights had a peculiar hoary aspect that made this tree seem more intensely alive than others, more conscious of my presence and watchful of me.

I never spoke of these feelings to others, not even to my mother, notwithstanding that she was always in perfect sympathy with me with regard to my love of nature. The reason of my silence was, I think, my powerlessness to convey in words what I felt, but I imagine it would be correct to describe the sensation experienced on those moonlight nights among the trees as similar to the feeling a person would have if visited by a supernatural being, if he was perfectly convinced that it was there in his presence, albeit silent and unseen, intently regarding him, and divining every thought in his mind. He would be thrilled to the marrow, but not terrified if he knew that it would take no visible shape nor speak to him out of the silence. . . .

Far Away and Long Ago: a History of my Early Life, 1918.

Silas Told

WHEN I was in petticoats, my sister Dulcybella and I wandered into the woods and fields, fixing ourselves under the hedges, conversing about God and happiness; so that at times I have been transported in such a measure with heavenly bliss, that whether in the body or out of the body, I could not tell: this happiness attended me for a few years.

Once, when we were very young, we wandered into Kingswood, and lost ourselves in the woods, and were in the utmost consternation, lest we should be devoured by the wild beasts; but quickly the kind providence of God permitted a large dog to come behind us; although no house was within a mile, yet the dog drove us clear out of the wood to a place we knew, and never barked at us. And when we now looked around to behold the dog, he was not to be seen. Being heedless, we wandered again into the woods, and were a second time bewildered, and in greater perplexity than before; when on a sudden, looking round, we beheld the same dog making towards us, and he came directly upon us; and we, being much terrified, ran from him, until we got a second time into our knowledge; nor did he leave us till we were driven by him where we could not come into any more labyrinths. I then turned about to look for the dog, but saw no more of him, although we were upon an open common. Surely this was the Lord's doing, and it is marvellous in our eyes.

. . . When I was about twelve years of age, I was more acquainted with divine things, but not with myself as a sinner. Sitting one day, reading the *Pilgrim's Progress,* I suddenly laid down my book, leaned my right elbow on my knee, with my hand supporting my head, and meditated in the most solemn manner upon the awfulness of eternity. Suddenly I was struck as with a hand on the top of my head, which affected my whole frame; the blow was immediately followed by a voice, with these words, "Dark! dark! dark!" and although it alarmed me prodigiously, yet upon recovering from so sudden a motion, I found myself broad awake in the world of sin. Notwithstanding all my former happiness, I now found nothing could give me satisfaction; nor could I ever rest satisfied about my salvation, as temptations from the world, the flesh and the devil were ever besetting me.

The Life of Mr Silas Told, written by himself, 1786.

Thomas Holcroft

I KNOW of nothing that tends so much as the anecdotes of childhood, when faithfully recorded, to guide the philosopher through that abstruse but important labyrinth, the gradations that lead to the full stature, peculiar form, temperament, character, and qualities of the man. I am therefore anxious to recount all those concerning myself, which I suppose may conduce to this purpose. . . .

The first place I distinctly remember myself, was London, where I have a faint notion of having been among boys with their school-books. Whether I was sent to school for a week or two, while my father and mother were adjusting their affairs, and preparing for their new career, is more than I can affirm or deny; although I have no recollection of acquiring any knowledge, a thing which, before this, had begun to make a strong impression on me. If I were really sent to school, it must have been for a very short time, nor could I have been provided with books or other means of improvement. And indeed my father was so straitened in his circumstances, that my mother very soon agreed to turn pedlar, having a basket with pins, needles, tape, garters and other small haberdashery on her arm, and hawked them through the outskirts and neighbourhood of London, while I trotted after her. I might at first perhaps feel some disgust at this employment; but use soon reconciled me to it, as the following anecdote will show.

I cannot say what my father's employment was, while I and my mother were, what they call emphatically, *tramping* the villages, to hawk our pedlary. It may be presumed, however, that it was not very lucrative, for he soon after left it, and he and my mother went into the country, hawking their small wares, and dragging me after them. They went first to Cambridge, and afterwards, as their hope of success led them, traversed the neighbouring villages. Among these we came to one which I thought most remarkably clean, well built, and unlike villages in general: my father said it was the handsomest in the kingdom. We must have been very poor, for here it was that I was either encouraged, or commanded, one day to go by myself, from house to house, and beg. Young as I was, I had considerable readiness in making out a story, and on this day, my little inventive faculties shone forth with much brilliancy. I told one story at one house, another at another, and continued to vary my tale just as the suggestions arose: the consequence of which was, that I moved the good country people exceedingly. One called me a poor fatherless child: another exclaimed, what a pity! I had so much sense! a third patted my head, and prayed God to preserve me, that I might make a good man. And most of them contributed either by scraps of meat, farthings, bread and cheese, or other homely offers, to enrich me, and send me away with my pockets loaded. I joyfully brought as much of my stores as I could carry to the place of rendezvous my parents had appointed, where I astonished them by again reciting the false tales I had so readily invented. My father, whose passions were easily aroused, felt no little conflict of mind as I proceeded. I can now, in imagination, see the working of his features. "God bless the boy! I never heard the like!" Then turning to my mother, he exclaimed with great earnestness, "This must not be! the poor child will become a commonplace liar! A hedge-side rogue! He will learn to pilfer!—Turn a confirmed vagrant!—Go on the highway when he is older, and get hanged! He shall never go on such errands again."

How fortunate for me in this respect that I had such a father! He was driven by extreme poverty, restless anxiety, and a brain too prone to sanguine expectation, into many absurdities, which were the harbingers of fresh misfortunes, but he had as much integrity and honesty of heart as perhaps any man in the kingdom, who had no greater advantages. It pleases me now to recollect that, though I had a consciousness that my talents could keep my parents from want, I had a still stronger sense of the justice of my father's remarks. I had not only read and remembered the consequences of good and evil, as they are pointed out in the Scriptures, but I had also become acquainted with some of the renowned heroes of fable; and to be a liar, a rogue, and get hanged, did not square well with the confused ideas I had either of goodness or greatness, or with my notions of a hero.

Memoirs of Thomas Holcroft, 1816.

Samuel Johnson

1711–12. This year in Lent '12, I was taken to London, to be touched for the evil by Queen Anne. My mother was at Nicholson's, the famous bookseller, in Little Britain. Though then with child, she concealed her pregnancy, that she might not be hindered from the journey. I always retained some memory of this journey, though I was then but thirty months old. I remembered a little dark room behind the kitchen, where the pack-weight fell through a hole in the floor, into which I once slipped my leg.

SAMUEL JOHNSON

I seem to remember, that I played with a string and a ball, which my cousin Isaac Johnson gave me; and that there was a cat with a white collar, and a dog, called Chops, that leaped over a stick, but I know not whether I remember the thing, or the talk of it.

I remember a boy crying at the palace when I went to be touched. Being asked "On which side of the shop was the counter?" I answered, "On the left from the entrance," many years after, and spoke, not by guess, but by memory. We went in the stage-coach, and returned in the waggon, as my mother said, because my cough was violent. The hope of saving a few shillings was no slight motive; for she, not having been accustomed to money, was afraid of such expenses as now seem very small. She sewed two guineas in her petticoat, lest she should be robbed.

We were troublesome to the passengers; but to suffer such inconveniences in the stage-coach was common in those days to persons in much higher rank. I was sick; one woman fondled me, the other was disgusted. My mother bought me a small silver cup and spoon, marked SAM. J., lest if they had been marked S.J., which was her name, they should, upon her death, have been taken from me. She bought me a speckled linen frock, which I knew afterwards by the name of my London frock. The cup was one of the last pieces of plate which dear Tetty sold in our distress. I have now the spoon. She bought at the same time two tea-spoons, and till my manhood she had no more.

An account of the Life of Samuel Johnson from his birth to his eleventh year, written by himself.

23

S. T. Coleridge

FROM October 1775 to October 1778. These three years I continued at the Reading School, because I was too little to be trusted among my Father's schoolboys. After breakfast I had a halfpenny given me, with which I bought three cakes at the baker's shop close by the school of my old mistress; and these were my dinner every day except Saturday and Sunday, when I used to dine at home, and wallowed in a beef and pudding dinner. I am remarkably fond of beans and bacon; and this fondness I attribute to my Father's giving me a penny for having eaten a large quantity of beans one Saturday. For the other boys did not like them, and, as it was an economic food, my Father thought my attachment to it ought to be encouraged. He was very fond of me, and I was my Mother's darling; in consequence of which I was very miserable. For Molly, who had nursed my brother Francis, and was immoderately fond of him, hated me because my Mother took more notice of me than of Frank; and Frank hated me because my Mother gave me now and then a bit of cake when he had none—quite forgetting that for one bit of cake which I had and he had not, he had twenty sops in the pan, and pieces of bread and butter with sugar on them from Molly, from whom I only received thumps and ill names.

So I became fretful, and timorous, and a tell-tale; and the schoolboys drove me from play, and were always tormenting me. And hence I took no pleasure in boyish sports, but read incessantly. I read through all the gilt-cover little books that could be had at that time, and likewise all the uncovered books of Tom Hickathrift, Jack the Giant Killer and the like. And I used to lie by the wall, and mope; and my spirits used to come upon me suddenly, and in a flood;—and then I was accustomed to run up and down the churchyard, and act over again all I had been reading on the docks, the nettles, and the rank grass. At six years of age I remember to have read Belisarius, Robinson Crusoe, and Philip Quarles; and then I found the Arabian Nights' Entertainments, one tale of which (the tale of a man who was compelled to seek for a pure virgin,) made so deep an impression on me, (I had read it in the evening while my mother was at her needle,) that I was haunted by spectres, whenever I was in the dark; and I distinctly recollect the anxious and fearful eagerness with which I used to watch the window where the book lay, and when the sun came upon it, I would seize it, carry it by the wall, and bask, and read. My father found out the effect which these books had produced, and burnt them.

So I became a dreamer, and acquired an indisposition to all bodily activity; and I was fretful, and inordinately passionate; and as I could not play at anything, and was slothful, I was despised and hated by the boys: and because I could read and spell, and had, I may truly say, a memory and understanding forced into almost unnatural ripeness, I was flattered and wondered at by all the old women. And so I became very vain, and despised most of the boys who were at all near my own age, and before I was eight years old I was a *character*. Sensibility, imagination, vanity, sloth, and feelings of deep and bitter contempt for almost all who traversed the orbit of my understanding, were even then prominent and manifest.

A letter written on October 9th, 1807,
to Thomas Poole of Nether Stowey.

Lucy Hutchinson

MY mother, while she was with child of me, dreamt that she was walking in the garden with my father, and that a star came down into her hand, with other circumstances which, though I have often heard, I minded not enough to remember perfectly; only my father told her, her dream signified she should have a daughter of some extraordinary eminency; which thing, like such vain prophecies, wrought as far as it could its own accomplishment; for my father and mother, fancying me then beautiful, and more than ordinarily apprehensive, applied all their cares and spared no cost to improve me in my education, which procured me the admiration of those that flattered my parents. By the time I was four years old I read English perfectly, and having a great memory, I was carried to sermons, and while I was very young could remember and repeat them so exactly, and being caressed, the love of praise tickled me, and made me attend more heedfully.

When I was about seven years of age, I remember I had at one time eight tutors in several qualities, languages, music, dancing, writing and needlework; but my genius was quite averse from all but my book, and that I was so eager of that my mother, thinking it prejudiced my health, would moderate me in it; yet this rather animated me than kept me back, and every moment I could steal from my play I would employ in any book I could find, when my own were locked up from me. After dinner and supper I still had an hour allowed me to play, and then I would steal into some hole or other to read. My father would have me learn Latin, and I was so eager that I outstripped my brothers who were at school, although my father's chaplain that was my tutor was a pitiful dull fellow. My brothers, who had a great deal of wit, had some emulation at the progress I made in my

LUCY HUTCHINSON

learning, which very well pleased my father, though my mother would have been contented I had not so wholly addicted myself to that as to neglect my other qualities. As for music and dancing, I profited very little in them, and would never practise my lute or harpsichords but when my masters were with me; and for my needle, I absolutely hated it. Play among other children I despised, and when I was forced to entertain such as came to visit me, I tired them with more grave instruction than their mothers, and plucked all their babies to pieces, and kept the children in such awe that they were glad when I entertained myself with elder company. . . .

Memoirs of the Life of Colonel Hutchinson . . . written by his widow Lucy . . . To which is prefixed the Life of Mrs Hutchinson, written by herself.

C. M. Yonge

I WAS repressed when I was troublesome, made to be obedient or to suffer for it, and was allowed few mere indulgences in eating or drinking, and no holidays. And yet I say it deliberately, that except for my occasional longings for a sister, no one ever had a happier or more joyous childhood than mine. I have since had reason to know that I was a very pretty and clever child, or at any rate that my mother thought so, but I really never knew whether I was not ugly. I know I thought myself so, and I was haunted occasionally by doubts whether I were not deficient, till I was nearly grown up. My mother said afterwards that I once asked her if I was pretty, and she replied that all young creatures were, i.e. the little pigs. Once when someone praised my chestnut curls, I set everyone laughing by replying indignantly, "You flatter me", having my head full of the flattering

27

lady in Miss Edgeworth's *Frank*. Great hazel eyes, and thick, rich, curling hair, cut rather short, were my best points, for my skin was always brown, and never had much colour.

My nature was eager, excitable, and at that time passionate. The worst passions I remember were excited by a housemaid named Sarah, who used to sit at work in the nursery, and beg my nurse Mason to repeat "the last dying speech and confession of poor Puss", because I could not bear that doleful ditty, and used to stamp and roll on the floor to put a stop to it. Sarah was very good-natured, though; she gave me a doll, and when I made a flight of steps to jump down—a chest of drawers, a chair, and a stool—she followed my lead, and jumped with such effect that all the legs of the stool spread out flat on the floor. I think it was found out that she was not a safe companion for me, for she did not stay long.

My nursery would frighten a modern mother. It was like a little passage room, at the back of the house, with a birch-tree just before the window, a wooden crib for me, and a turn-up press bed for my nurse; and it also answered the purpose of workroom for the maids. But I did not live much in it. I was one of the family breakfast party, and dined at luncheon so early that I cannot remember when I began, and never ate in the nursery except my supper. Breakfast and supper were alike dry bread and milk. I so much disliked the hot bowl of boiled milk and cubes of bread that I was allowed to have mine separately, but butter was thought unwholesome, and I believe it would have been so, for I never have been able to eat it regularly. As to eggs, ham, jam, and all the rest, no one dreamt of giving them to children. Indeed my mother made a great point of never letting me think that it was any hardship to see other people eating of what I did not partake, and I have been grateful for the habits she gave me ever since.

I remember my indignation when a good-natured housemaid, who thought me cruelly treated, brought up a plateful of slices with the buttered side downwards. With conscious pride and honour, I denounced the deceit. I wonder whether the strict obedience edified her, or whether she thought me a horrid little ungrateful tell-tale.

Charlotte Mary Yonge: Life and Letters,
by C. R. Coleridge, 1903.

Mary Robinson

ALL the offspring of my parents were, in their infancy, uncommonly handsome, excepting myself. The boys were fair and lusty, with auburn hair, light blue eyes, and countenances peculiarly animated and lovely. I was swarthy; my eyes were singularly large in proportion to my face, which was small and round, exhibiting features peculiarly marked with the most pensive and melancholy cast.

The great difference betwixt my brothers and myself, in point of personal beauty, tended much to endear me to my parents, particularly to my father, whom I strongly resembled. The early propensities of my life were tinctured with romantic and singular characteristics; some of which I shall here mention, as proofs that the mind is never to be diverted from its original bent; and that every event of my life has been more or less marked by the progressive evils of a too acute sensibility.

The nursery in which I passed my hours of infancy was so near the great aisle of the Minster, that the organ, which re-echoed its deep tones, accompanied by the chanting of the choristers, was distinctly heard both at morning and evening service. I remember with what pleasure I used to listen, and how much I was delighted whenever I was permitted to sit on the winding steps which led from the aisle to the cloisters. I can at this moment recall to memory the sensations I then experienced; the tones that seemed to thrill through my heart, the longing which I felt to unite my feeble voice to the full anthem, and the

29

awful, though sublime, impression which the church service never failed to make upon my feelings. While my brothers were playing on the green before the Minster, the servant who attended us has often, by my earnest entreaties, suffered me to remain beneath the great eagle which stood in the centre of the aisle, to support the book from which the clergyman read the lessons of the day; and nothing could keep me away, even in the coldest seasons, but the stern looks of an old man, whom I named Black John from the colour of his beard and complexion, and whose occupations within the sacred precincts were those of a bell-ringer and sexton.

Memoirs of Mrs Mary Robinson, 1801.

John Ruskin

IT is perhaps already time to mark what advantage and mischief, by the chances of life up to seven years old, had been irrevocably determined for me.

I will first count my blessings (as a not unwise friend once recommended me to do, continually; whereas I have a bad trick of always numbering the thorns in my fingers and not the bones in them).

And for the best and truest beginning of all blessings, I had been taught the perfect meaning of Peace, in thought, act, and word.

I had never heard my father's or mother's voice once raised in any question with each other; nor seen an angry, or even slightly hurt or offended, glance in the eyes of either. I had never heard a servant scolded; nor even suddenly, passionately, or in any severe manner, blamed. I had never seen a moment's trouble or disorder in any household matter; nor anything whatever either done in a hurry, or undone in due time. I had no conception of such a feeling as anxiety; my father's occasional vexation in the afternoons, when he had only got an order for twelve butts after expecting one for fifteen, was never manifested to *me*; and itself related only to the question whether his name would be a step higher or lower in the year's list of sherry exporters; for he never spent more than half his income, and therefore found himself little incommoded by occasional variations in the total of it. I had never done any wrong that I knew of—beyond occasionally delaying the commitment to heart of some improving sentence, that I might watch a wasp on the window pane, or a bird in the cherry tree; and I had never seen grief.

Next to this quite priceless gift of Peace, I had received the perfect understanding of the natures of Obedience and Faith. I obeyed word, or lifted finger, of father or mother, simply as a ship her helm; not only without idea of resistance, but receiving the direction as a part of my own life and force, a helpful law, as necessary to me in every moral action as the law of gravity in leaping. And my practice in Faith was soon complete: nothing was ever promised me that was not given; nothing ever threatened me that was not inflicted, and nothing ever told me that was not true.

Peace, obedience, faith; these three for chief good; next to these, the habit of fixed attention with both eyes and mind— on which I will not further enlarge at this moment, this being the main practical faculty of my life, causing Mazzini to say of me, in conversation authentically reported, a year or two before his death, that I had "the most analytic mind in Europe." An opinion in which, so far as I am acquainted with Europe, I am myself eminently disposed to concur.

Lastly, an extreme perfection in palate and all other bodily senses, given by the utter prohibition of cake, wine, comfits, or, except in carefullest restriction, fruit; and by fine preparation of what food was given me. Such I esteem the main blessings of my childhood;—next, let me count the equally dominant calamities.

First, that I had nothing to love.

My parents were—in a sort—visible powers of nature to me, no more loved than the sun and the moon; only I should have been annoyed and puzzled if either of them had gone out; (how much, now, when both are darkened!)—still less did I love God; not that I had any quarrel with Him, or fear of Him; but simply found what people told me was His service, disagreeable; and what people told me was His book, not entertaining. I had no companions to quarrel with, neither; nobody to assist, and nobody to thank. Not a servant was ever allowed to do anything for me, but what it was their duty to do; and why should I have been grateful to the cook for cooking, or the gardener for gardening—when the one dared not give me a baked potato without asking leave, and the other would not leave my ants' nests alone, because they made the walks untidy? The evil consequence of all this was not, however, what might perhaps have been expected, that I grew up selfish or unaffectionate; but that, when affection did come, it came with violence utterly rampant and unmanageable, at least by me, who never before had anything to manage.

For (second of chief calamities) I had nothing to endure. Danger or pain of any kind I knew not: my strength was never exercised, my patience never tried, and my courage never fortified. Not that I was ever afraid of anything,—either ghosts, thunder, or beasts; and one of the nearest approaches to insubordination which I was ever tempted into as a child, was in passionate effort to get leave to play with the lion's cubs in Wombwell's menagerie.

Thirdly. I was taught no precision nor etiquette of manners; it was enough if, in the little society we saw, I remained unobtrusive, and replied to a question without shyness: but the shyness came later, and increased as I grew conscious of the rudeness arising from the want of social discipline, and found it impossible to acquire, in advanced life, dexterity in any bodily activity, skill in any pleasing accomplishment, or ease and tact in ordinary behaviour.

Last, and chief of evils. My judgment of right and wrong,

and powers of independent action, were left entirely undeveloped; because the bridle and blinkers were never taken off me. Children should have their times of being off duty, like soldiers; and when once the obedience, if required, is certain, the little creature should be very early put for periods of practice in complete command of itself; set on the bare-backed horse of its own will, and left to break it by its own strength. But the ceaseless authority exercised over my own youth left me, when cast out at last into the world, unable for some time to do more than drift with its vortices.

My present verdict, therefore, on the general tenor of my education at that time, must be, that it was at once too formal and too luxurious; leaving my character, at the most important moment for its construction, cramped indeed, but not disciplined; and only by protection innocent instead of by practice virtuous. My mother saw this herself, and but too clearly, in later years; and whenever I did anything wrong, stupid, or hard-hearted,— (and I have done many things that were all three,)—always said, "It is because you were too much indulged."

Praeterita : Outlines of Scenes and Thoughts perhaps worthy of memory in my past life, 1885–1889.

Augustus Hare

As Uncle Julius was never captivating to children, it is a great pity that he was turned into an additional bugbear, by being always sent for to whip me when I was naughty. These executions generally took place with a riding-whip, and looking back dispassionately through the distance of years, I am conscious that, for a delicate child, they were a great deal too severe. I always screamed dreadfully in anticipation of them, but bore them without a sound or a tear. I remember one very hot summer's day, when I had been very naughty over my lessons, that Uncle Julius was summoned. He arrived, and I was sent upstairs to "prepare". Then, as I knew I was going to be whipped anyway, I thought I might as well do something horrible to be whipped *for*, and as soon as I reached the head of the stairs, gave three of the most awful, appalling and eldrich shrieks that ever were heard at Hurstmonceaux. Then I fled for my life. Through the nursery was a small bedroom, in which Lea slept, and here I knew that a large black travelling "imperial" was kept under the bed. Under the bed I crawled, and wedged myself into the narrow space behind the imperial, between it and the wall. I was only just in time. In an instant all the household—mother, uncle, servants—were in motion, and a search was on foot all over the house. I turn cold still when I remember the agony of fright with which I heard Uncle Julius enter the nursery, and then, with which, through a chink, I could see his large feet moving about the very room in which I was. He *looked under the bed*, but he saw only a large black box. I held my breath, motionless, and he turned away.

I lay under the bed for an hour—stifling—agonised. Then all sounds died away, and I knew that the search in the house was over, and that they were searching the garden. At last my curiosity would no longer allow me to be still, and I crept from under the bed and crawled to the window. Every dark shrub, every odd corner was being ransacked. The whole household and the gardeners were engaged in the pursuit. At last I could see by their actions—for I could not hear words—that a dreadful idea had presented itself. In my paroxysms I had rushed down the steep bank, and tumbled or thrown myself into the pond! I saw my mother look very wretched and Uncle Julius try to calm her. At last they sent for people to drag the pond. Then I could bear my dear mother's expression no longer, and from my high window, I gave a little hoot. Instantly all was changed; Lea rushed upstairs to embrace me; there was great talking and excitement, and while it was going on, Uncle Julius was called away, and everyone forgot that I had not been whipped! That, however, was the only time I ever escaped.

In the most literal sense, and in every other, I was "brought up at the point of the rod." My dearest mother was so afraid of over-indulgence that she always went to the opposite extreme: and her constant habits of self-examination made her detect the slightest act of especial kindness into which she had been betrayed, and instantly determine not to repeat it. Nevertheless, I loved her most passionately, and many tearful fits, for which I was severely punished as fits of naughtiness, were really caused by anguish at the thought that I had displeased her or been a trouble to her. From never daring to express my wishes in words, which she would have thought a duty to meet by an immediate refusal, I early became a coward as to concealing what I really desired. I remember once, in my longing for childish companionship, so intensely desiring that the little Coshams—a family of children who lived in the parish—might come to play with me, that I entreated that they might come to have tea in the summer-house on my Hurstmonceaux birthday (the day of my adoption), and that the mere request was not only refused, but so punished that I never dared to express a wish to play with any child again.

The Story of my Life, 1896.

Edmund Gosse

IT was about the date of my sixth birthday that I did something very naughty, some act of direct disobedience, for which my Father, after a solemn sermon, chastised me, sacrificially, by giving me several cuts with a cane. This action was justified, as everything he did was justified, by reference to Scripture— "Spare the rod and spoil the child." I suppose that there are some children, of a sullen and lymphatic temperament, who are smartened up and made more wide-awake by a whipping. It is largely a matter of convention, the exercise being endured (I am told) with pride by the infants of our aristocracy, but not tolerated by the lower classes. I am afraid that I proved my inherent vulgarity by being made, not contrite or humble, but furiously angry by this caning. I cannot account for the flame of rage which it awakened in my bosom. My dear, excellent Father had beaten me, not very severely, without ill-temper, and with the most genuine desire to improve me. But he was not well-advised, especially so far as the "dedication to the Lord's service" was concerned. This same "dedication" had ministered to my vanity, and there are some natures which are not improved by being humiliated. I have to confess with shame that I went about the house for some days with a murderous hatred of my Father locked within my bosom. He did not suspect that the chastisement had not been wholly efficacious, and he bore me no malice; so that after a while, I forgot and thus forgave him. But I do not regard physical punishment as a wise element in the education of proud and sensitive children.

My theological misdeeds culminated, however, in an act so puerile and preposterous that I should not venture to record it if it did not throw some glimmering of light on the subject which I have proposed to myself in writing these pages. My mind continued to dwell on the mysterious question of prayer. It puzzled me greatly to know why, if we were God's children, and if he was watching over us by night and day, we might not supplicate for toys and sweets and smart clothes as well as for the conversion of the heathen. Just at this juncture, we had a special service at the Room, at which our attention was particularly called to what we always spoke of as "the field of missionary labour". The East was represented among "the saints" by an excellent Irish peer, who had in his early youth, converted and married a lady of colour; this Asiatic shared in our Sunday morning meetings, and was an object of helpless terror to me; I shrank from her amiable caresses, and vaguely identified her with a personage much spoken of in our family circle, the "Personal Devil".

All these matters drew my thoughts to the subject of idolatry, which was severely censured at the missionary meeting. I cross-examined my Father very closely as to the nature of this sin, and pinned him down to the categorical statement that idolatry consisted in praying to any one or anything but God himself. Wood and stone, in the words of the hymn, were peculiarly liable to be bowed down to by the heathen in their blindness. I pressed my Father further on this subject, and he assured me that God would be very angry, and would signify His anger, if any one, in a Christian country, bowed down to wood and stone. I cannot recall why I was so pertinacious on this subject, but I remember that my Father became a little restive under my cross-examination. I determined, however, to test the matter for myself, and one morning, when my parents were safely out of the house, I prepared for the great act of heresy. I was in the morning-room on the ground floor, where, with much labour, I hoisted a small chair on to the table close to the window. My heart was now beating as if it would leap out of my side, but I pursued my experiment. I knelt down on the carpet in front of the table and looking up I said my daily prayer in a loud voice, only substituting the adress "O Chair!" for the habitual one.

Having carried this act of idolatry safely through, I waited to see what would happen. It was a fine day, and I gazed up at the slip of white sky above the houses opposite, and expected something to appear in it. God would certainly exhibit his anger in some terrible form, and would chastise my impious and wilful action. I was very much alarmed, but still more excited; I breathed the high, sharp air of defiance. But nothing happened; there was not a cloud in the sky, not an unusual sound in the street. Presently I was quite sure that nothing would happen. I had committed idolatry, flagrantly and deliberately, and God did not care.

The result of this ridiculous act was not to make me question the existence and power of God; those were forces which I did not dream of ignoring. But what it did was to lessen still further my confidence in my Father's knowledge of the Divine mind. My Father had said, positively, that if I worshipped a thing made of wood, God would manifest his anger. I had worshipped a chair, made (or partly made) of wood, and God had made no sign whatever. My Father, therefore, was not really acquainted with the Divine practice in cases of idolatry. And with that, dismissing the subject, I dived again into the unplumbed depths of the "Penny Cyclopedia."

Father and Son, 1907.

R. D. Owen

BUT aside from religious convictions and the desire to atone for my sins urging me on, there was that organ of self-esteem, hereditary perhaps, the size of which in my brain the great phrenologist had detected. Under its influence I could not get away from the resolve to convert my father. I say the resolve to *convert him,* not to *attempt his conversion;* for so I put it to myself, nothing doubting.

I don't think I had any clear conception what a mission is. Yet I had a vague idea that God had chosen me to be the instrument of my father's salvation, so that he might not be sent to hell when he died.

I was mightily pleased with myself when this idea presented itself, and I set about preparing for the task before me. Summoning to my recollection all my mother's strongest arguments, I arranged them in the order in which I proposed to bring them forward. Then I imagined my father's replies; already anticipating my own triumph and my mother's joy when I should have brought my father to confess his errors and repent. But I said not a word of my intentions to her or to any one. The joyful surprise was to be complete.

I recollect, to this day, the spot on which I commenced my long-projected undertaking. It was on a path which skirted, on the farther side, the lawn in front of our house and led to the garden. I could point out the very tree we were passing when—with some misgivings, now that it was to be put to the test—I sounded my father by first asking him what he thought about Jesus Christ. His reply was to the effect that I would do well to heed his teachings, especially those relating to charity and to our loving one another.

This was well enough, as far as it went; but it did not at all satisfy me. So, with some trepidation, I put the question direct, whether my father disbelieved that Christ was the Son of God?

He looked a little surprised and did not answer immediately. "Why do you ask that question, my son?" he said at last.

"Because I am sure—" I began eagerly.

"That he *is* God's Son?" asked my father, smiling.

"Yes, I am."

"Did you ever hear of the Mahometans?" said my father, while I had paused to collect my proofs.

I replied that I had heard of such a people who lived somewhere far off.

"Do you know what their religion is?"

"No."

"They believe that Christ is not the Son of God, but that another person, called Mahomet, was God's chosen prophet."

"Do they not believe the Bible?" asked I, somewhat aghast.

"No. Mahomet wrote a book called the Koran; and Mahometans believe it to be the word of God. That book tells them that God sent Mahomet to preach the gospel to them, and to save their souls."

Wonders crowded fast upon me. A rival Bible and a rival Saviour! Could it be? I asked, "Are you *quite* sure this is true, papa?"

"Yes, my dear, I am quite sure."

"But I suppose there are very few Mahometans; not near, *near* so many of them as of Christians."

"Do you call Catholics Christians, Robert?"

"O no, papa. The Pope is Antichrist."

My father smiled. "Then by Christians you mean Protestants?"

"Yes."

"Well, there are many more Mahometans than Protestants in the world; about a hundred and forty million Mahometans, and less than a hundred million Protestants."

"I thought almost everybody believed in Christ, as mamma does."

"There are probably twelve hundred millions of people in the world. So out of every twelve persons only one is a Protestant. Are you *quite* sure that the one is right and the eleven wrong?"

My creed, based on authority, was toppling. I had no answer ready. During the rest of the walk I remained almost silent, engrossed with new ideas, and replying chiefly in monosyllables when spoken to.

And so ended this notable scheme of mine for my father's conversion.

Threading my Way: twenty-seven years of autobiography, 1874.

Alexander Somerville

B u t to return to the time of the radicals of 1819, and the rumours that came to Birnyknows school, that "they were coming." The term "ragged radicals" was a common one in the newspapers of that time, and the boys who heard their fathers read the newspapers or talk of the news, brought this name of reproach to the school. It was suggested one day by some of them, that an excellent play might be got up in the Eel Yards, a meadow with some large trees in it, if the scholars divided themselves into soldiers and radicals. As the soldiers were the most respectable in the eyes of the better dressed sons of farmers and tradesmen, and as they took the lead in eveything, they made themselves soldiers; and, in addition to that, took upon themselves to pick out those who were to be radicals. This was done according to the quality of the clothes worn, and I, consequently, found myself declared to be a radical. The first day's play passed with no greater disasters to me than the brim torn from an infirm hat which I wore, my trousers split up, all the buttons torn from my waistcoat, and my neck stretched considerably on the way to strangulation. For being a radical who seemed inclined to look upon the treatment I received as too serious for play, I was condemned to be hanged. It happened that the clothes I wore were not of the usual corduroy worn by the sons of farm labourers and always worn by me, save in that year. Mine had been remade the year before from some cast-off clothes given a year or two before that to the brother next to me in age by his master. There was a brown coat which had been reduced in size, but it was still too big for me; trousers which had once been of a very light-blue or grey; and the infirm hat already mentioned, which came to our family I do not remember precisely how; but it had so broad a brim at first, that my mother cut away part of it to let me see from below it, and still it was so broad that some of the boys nicknamed me after some people whom I had never seen nor heard of, but who were said to wear broad-brimmed hats. These clothes having been old when I got them, and having been worn by me all the summer in the woods herding the cows, and all the autumn, they were not in sound condition. But my poor mother always kept them patched up; and I never once went out then or any time, with an open rent or a worn hole in my clothes. As she spun wool for stockings, and lint for shirts, herself, and my father knitted stockings, and my sisters made shirts, I was equal in those articles to any one in the school; and I was only so badly clothed otherwise because the second year was running on between my father and a master for whom he then worked without a settlement of accounts; the said master allowing my father to get oats for meal, and barley and beans for bread, but being sadly embarrassed as a landowner, with his land mortgaged—not able at that time to pay up the arrears of wages.

When I went home on that first evening of my ragged radical-ship, my poor mother stood aghast, lifted her hands, and said in a tone of despair, "What shall I do with those rags?" They were stripped off, I got an early supper and was sent to bed, while she began to mend them—putting in a piece here and a piece there, sewing up a rent, darning the worn holes, and ending some hours after midnight, not far from the usual hour of rising from bed, by sewing the luckless brim on my infirm hat. Her motherly affection for me, and natural pride in the good appearance of her family, had led her to suggest to my father that I should not be sent to school until we had got the "siller" we were waiting for to get new clothes. But my father, though not less affectionate, and not less anxious about the appearance of his family, was stern upon that point. "If the laddie lives to be a man," said he, "he will need his education, and more than we can give him. If I had got schooling myself, as I am trying to give to all my sons, it would have helped me through the world more easily than I have got through. The laddie must go to school."

So I went to the school, my mother begging of me, with tears in her eyes, not to get my clothes torn again, else it would kill her to see me in such rags, and to have to sit up every night to mend them. But "soldiers and radicals" was again the play, and again I was the radical upon whom the greatest number of soldiers concentrated their warfare. They had seen me thrashed by the schoolmaster until I was blistered, without crying or shedding a tear, which made them think I could stand any amount of punish-ment or torment, without feeling it; in short, I was believed to be a great stubborn lad, who had no feeling in him. Had they seen me after leaving my mother that morning, and carrying her injunction with me, in a heart that was bursting with her words, they would have seen whether I had tears in me or not, and whether they would not come out.

As soon as I made my appearance, the cry of "ragged radical" was raised; the soldiers charged on me, and knocked my infirm hat over my eyes with my head through the crown of it. Some laid hold of me by the feet to carry me off to be hanged and beheaded, *as the real law upon the real radicals had taught them to imitate in play*. I made a violent effort to free myself, and the rents of yesterday, which my mother had so carefully sewed, broke open afresh. The hat I raised from where it had sunk over my face, and saw part of the brim in the hands of a lad who was a kind of king of the school, or cock of the walk, with some of my poor mother's threads hanging from it. He was older than I, and was a fighter. I had never fought, nor had heard of two human beings going together to fight, until I came to that school. Yet neither had I heard of the divine principle of forbearance and forgiveness, as regards blows upon the body, and the laceration of feelings worse than blows upon the body—my father, who gave me many good precepts, never having contemplated the possibility of my being a fighting boy. (My child, you will be brought up where there are policemen and law, lawyers and magistrates to take your part if you are injured; never raise your own hand against any one). But I was a strong boy for my age, and I had received very bad treatment. My honour and the remembrance of my affectionate mother's toils made me feel like a giant. I amazed the king of the school by giving him a blow on the face that laid him flat on his back, and amazed the onlookers by giving several of them as much with the same results. Not that I escaped without blows myself. I got many, but they were returned with principle and interest. Someone ran to the schoolmaster and told that I was thrashing "Master" Somebody, for he being a gentleman's son was called "Master", while I had to submit to a nickname, derived from the state of my clothes. The school was summoned at once, it being near the schoolhour in the morning. Some of those whose noses were bleeding ran to school with them in that state to let their disasters be seen. Another one and myself tried to get water to wash our faces, for mine was in as bad a condition as the worst of theirs; but the frost was so hard that we could not break the ice to get water, and at last were compelled to obey the repeated summons to school in the dreadful guise we were then in; my clothes being torn half off me in addition to the hideousness of the blood streaming from my face.

The schoolmaster stood with the *taws* ready to flagellate the moment I entered the school. He inquired who began the fight, and everyone named me. He at once ordered me to hold up my right hand, which I did, and received a violent cut on the edge of it, given with his whole strength. He ordered my left hand up, and up it went and received a cut of the same kind; then my right, which got what it got before; next my left, which also got what it got before; and so on he went until I had got six cuts (skults we called them) on each hand. He had a way of raising himself on his toes when the swung the heavy *taws* round his head, and came down on his feet with a spring, giving the cuts slantingly on the hand. He saw me resolved to take all he could give me without a tear, whereupon he began to cut at the back of my hands. I drew them behind me to save them, which seeing, he cut at the open places of my torn clothes, where my skin was visible; and always as I wriggled to one side to save those bare places, I exposed other bare places on the other side, which he aimed at with terrible certainty. After a time he pushed me before him, still thrashing me on the bare places, and on the head, until he got me to the farther end of the school, where the coals lay in a corner. He thrashed me until I got on the top of the coals. Here he ordered me to sit down and remain until he gave me liberty to leave that place, which he did not do until evening. The day was piercing cold. The house was an old place, with no furniture nor partition in it. I sat at the end farthest from the fireplace and near to the door, which was an old door that did not fit its place, and which allowed the wind to blow freely through. It blew through and about me as if it had been another schoolmaster, and was as partial to the farmers' sons, and as cruel to the ragged boys of farm labourers, as he was.

The Autobiography of a Working Man, 1848.

Expanding Horizons

—— ⊙ ——

WILLIAM COBBETT

JOHN CLARE

J. LEIGH HUNT

ROGER NORTH

JAMES LACKINGTON

CHARLOTTE CHARKE

JOSEPH ARCH

GEORGE WHITEFIELD

JOHN AUBREY

MARK PATTISON

ANTHONY TROLLOPE

HERBERT SPENCER

R. G. COLLINGWOOD

William Cobbett

AT eleven years of age my employment was clipping of box-edgings and weeding beds of flowers in the garden of the Bishop of Winchester, at the Castle of Farnham. I had always been fond of beautiful gardens; and a gardener, who had just come from the King's gardens at Kew, gave such a description of them as made me instantly resolve to work in these gardens. The next morning, without saying a word to anybody, off I set, with no clothes, except those upon my back, and thirteen halfpence in my pocket. I found that I must go to Richmond, and I accordingly went on, from place to place, inquiring my way thither. A long day (it was in June) brought me to Richmond in the afternoon. Two pennyworth of bread and cheese, and a pennyworth of small beer, which I had on the road, and one halfpenny that I had lost somewhere or other, left three pence in my pocket. With this for my whole fortune, I was trudging through Richmond, in my blue smock-frock and my red garters tied under my knees, when, staring about me, my eye fell upon a little book, in a bookseller's window: *Tale of a Tub*: price 3d. The title was so odd, that my curiosity was excited. I had the 3d. but, then, I could have no supper. In I went and got the little book, which I was so impatient to read, that I got over into a field, at the upper corner of Kew Gardens, where there stood a haystack. On the shady side of this, I sat down to read. The book was so different from anything that I had ever read before; it was something so new to my mind, that though I could not at all understand some of it, it delighted me beyond description; and it produced what I have always considered a sort of birth of intellect. I read on till it was dark, without any thought about supper or bed. When I could see no longer, I put my little book in my pocket, and tumbled down by the side of the stack, where I slept till the birds of Kew Garden awaked me in the morning; when off I started to Kew, reading my little book. The singularity of my dress, the simplicity of my manner, my confident and lively air, induced the gardener, who was a Scotchman, I remember, to give me victuals, find me lodging and set me to work . . .

Life and Adventures of Peter Porcupine, 1796.

John Clare

THERE I got into a habit of musing and muttering to one's self as pastime to divert melancholy, singing over things which I called songs, and attempting to describe scenes that struck me; 'tis irksome to a boy to be alone, and he is ready in such situations to snatch hold of any trifle to divert his loss of company, and make up for pleasanter amusements. For as my master was weak and unwell, he seldom went to work with me unless necessary, as ploughing etc. I always went by myself to weeding the grain, tending horses and such like. Once every week, I had to go for a bag of flour to Maxey, a village distant about two miles, as it was sold cheaper than at home, and as my mistress was an economist, she never lost sight of cheap pennyworths. In the short days of winter, it's often been dark ere I got home, and even bytimes dusk before I started. I was of a very timid disposition; the traditional registers of the village was uncommonly superstitious (gossips and grannys); and I had two or three haunted spots to pass. For it was impossible to go half a mile anywhere about the lordship where there had nothing been said to be seen by these old women or some one else in their younger days. Therefore I must in such extremities seize the best remedy I could to keep such things out of my head, as well as I could; so on these journeys I muttered over tales of my own fancy, contriving them into rhymes as well as my abilities was able. They was always romantic wanderings of sailors, soldiers etc, following them step by step from their starting out to their return; for I always lov'd to see a tale end happy, and as I had only myself to please, I always contrived that my taste should be suited in such matters.

Sometimes I was tracking my own adventures, as I wished they might be; going on from the plough to flail, to the easy chair of old age, reciting amorous intrigues (of meeting always good fortune, and marrying ladies etc). Hope was now budding, and its summer sky warmed me with thrilling extacy; and tho', however, romantic my story might be, I had always cautions fearful enough, no doubt, to keep ghosts and hobgoblins out of the question; what I did was to erase them, and not bring them to remembrance; tho' 'twas impossible. For as I pass'd those awful places, tho' I dare not look boldly up, my eye was warily on the watch, glegging under my hat at every stir of a leaf or murmur of the wind, and a quaking thistle was able to make me swoon with terror. I generally kept looking on the ground, and have been so taken with my story that I have gone muttering it over into the town, before I knew I got there.

(At the age of about thirteen, having come across a fragment of Thomson's *Seasons* he resolved to possess a copy of the book.)

On the next Sunday, I started to Stamford to buy Thomson, for I teazed my father out of the 1s. 6d., and would not let him have any peace till he consented to give it me; but when I got there, I was told by a young shop boy in the street (who had a book in his hand, which I found to be Collins' *Odes and Poems*) that the booksellers would not open the shop in a Sunday. This was a disappointment most strongly felt, and I returned home in very low spirits; but having to tend horses the next week, in company with other boys, I planned a scheme in secret to obtain my wishes by stealth, giving one of the boys a penny to keep my horses in my absence, with an additional penny to keep the secret.

I started off, and as we was generally soon with getting out our horses, that they might fill themselves before the flies was out,

I got to Stamford, I dare say, before a door had been opened, and loitered about the town for hours ere I could obtain my wishes. I at length got it, with an agreeable disappointment in return for my first, buying it for 6d. less than I propos'd, and never was I more pleased with a bargain than I was with this shilling purchase. On my return the sun got up, and it was a beautiful morning; I could not wait till I got back without reading it, and as I did not like to let anybody see me reading on the road of a working day, I clumb over the wall into Burghley Park, and nestled in a lawn at the wall side.

The scenery around me was uncommonly beautiful at that time of the year, and what with reading the book, and beholding the beauties of artful nature in the park, I got into a strain of descriptive rhyming on my journey home. This was *The Morning Walk*, the first thing I committed to paper. . . .

Sketches in the Life of John Clare, written by himself.

J. Leigh Hunt

I AM grateful to Christ Hospital for having bred me up in old cloisters, for its making me acquainted with the languages of Homer and Ovid, and for its having secured to me, on the whole, a well-trained and cheerful boyhood. It pressed no superstition upon me. It did not hinder my growing mind from making what excursions it pleased into the wide and healthy regions of general literature. I might buy as much Collins and Gray as I pleased, and get novels to my heart's content from the circulating libraries. There was nothing prohibited but what would have been prohibited by all good fathers; and everything was encouraged which would have been encouraged by the Steeles, and Addisons and Popes; by the Warburtons, and Atterburys, and Hoadleys. Boyer was a severe, nay, a cruel master; but age and reflection have made me sensible that I ought always to add my testimony to his being a laborious and a conscientious one. When his severity went beyond the mark, I believe he was always sorry for it: sometimes I am sure he was. He once (though the anecdote at first sight may look like a burlesque on the remark) knocked out one of my teeth with the back of a Homer, in a fit of impatience at my stammering. The tooth was a loose one, and I told him as much; but the blood rushed out as I spoke: he turned pale, and on my proposing to go out and wash the mouth, he said, "Go, child," in a tone of voice amounting to the paternal. Now, "Go, child," from Boyer, was worth a dozen tender speeches from anyone else; and it was felt that I had got an advantage over him, acknowledged by himself.

Autobiography: with reminiscences of
friends and contemporaries, 1850.

Roger North

HERE (the Free School at Bury St. Edmund's) I stayed two or three years, and was then removed to the Free School at Thetford, which was a most excellent air for health; and then furnished with an agreeable master. He was scholar enough, and withal mild and discreet. He had no fault but too much addicted to drinking company, which at last made him a sot and ended his days. But he used not to neglect his school, but take his cups when we took our liberty. Here I stayed till I was ready for the University, and first began here to be sensible of some tolerable capacity; for I came away with a schoolboy's conscience undefiled, never being assisted in any school exercise, but performed all myself. And though not of the prime of my rank, yet not contemptible, and might, my master used to say, have been better, were I not lazy, which he often laid in my dish. I must confess, in English I have borrowed from books whole sets of verses; but my luck was such that I had none but very mean ones to steal out of, such as *Poor Robin* and Quarles, which not being in my master's library, I was never discovered. Once, I remember, on a Restoration Day I had filched a copy from *Poor Robin* which at last concluded with a highflown passage—

But I
In perfect loyalty will live and die—

at which my master exclaimed and said I should be trusty Roger.

I was not very athletic, yet stood not out in any such exercise, but pleased myself more in manufactures and gimcracks, which was an indication of an inclination which ever did and will follow me. I had several manufactures going, as lanterns of paper, balls, thread purses, which brought in some money. I had got a trick to make fireworks, as serpents, which being strong bound, and the composition little abated with coal, would act very impetuously; but I could not make a rocket hold, for want of the skill to temper and take down from the composition, but all I offered at broke; yet I could make the serpents, being small and so bearing the force with a wand bound to them, rise as rockets. I got acquainted with artificers, and learnt to turn, which was a great diversion to me, because it produced somewhat neat, and well accommodated to several of the plays we had. There was lewd company among us, but I was not forward enough to be taken into their gang, though I, like others, was very desirous to come up to the state of manhood, most shewed, as I thought, by the conversation of women.

There was a navigable river in the town, which above the bridge branched into many brooks and scattered streams. This made us all expert boatmen, swimmers and fishers. We used to pass whole days naked; and once going to a sandy place to swim, a frolic carried us to Brandon, where, after example, I got drunk, and in the return must needs go swim again, but at first step fell over all into the water, being not in a condition to stand. The cold of the water made us all instantly sober, and after our pastime we returned home in good order.

There is a Saxon castle hill and three great ramparts round it, built, as I suppose, to defend the pass against the Mercian inroads. I had acquired a habit to run down from the summit of the hill to the bottom, and to stop or go swift as I would, which was done by keeping the body always perpendicular and using the point of the right heel to stop on, which sometimes would slide till it met a rub, but if not I kept the upright posture, which was always secure. This I could never teach any, and wondered at myself for it, being a sleight not ordinary.

Here it was that I began (as I said) to have a sense of myself. I was aspiring enough, and would have been in league with the capital boys, but had not a tour of address and confidence to be admitted, but kept in a middle order, and had my equals and inferiors, as well as superiors. I conceived a strange apprehension that I should prove a weak man, if not a fool, which showed I aimed at more than I found I could reach, and in this despondence I had no comfort but performing exercises without help. That did almost persuade me I should shift in other stations as well as that. I had, by the benefaction of several relations, a better cash than others, which made me an envy to the rest. This went partly in trade, which I hinted, and most in fruit, of which I was a most insatiable helluo. If fruit had been in any way hurtful, I had been poisoned. There was seldom a night when I did not eat a pennyworth of apples (and no small one) in bed before I slept, but this was in time of ripe apples, for green fruit I never could like, and surely ripe fruit is the best food for young folks.

Here I first knew what debt was, for this ingordigiousness of fruit having exhausted our stock, being good customers we found credit, and once was upon the score two shillings and sixence, which was a burden so heavy to a little man of honour that he declined ever after to be in like circumstances, and having cleared this by an expendient of old clothes, was firmly resolved in the matter.

Autobiography.

James Lackington

I HAD such good eyes, that I often read by the light of the moon, as my master would never permit me to take a candle into my room, and that prohibition I looked upon as a kind of persecution, but I always comforted myself with the thoughts of my being a dear child of God; and as such, that it was impossible for me to escape persecution from the children of the devil, which epithets I very *piously* applied to my good master and mistress. And so ignorantly and imprudently zealous (being a real Methodist) was I for the good of their precious souls, as sometimes to give them broad hints of it, and of the dangerous state they were in. . . . My good mistress wisely thought that a good stick was the best way of arguing with such an ignorant, infatuated boy as I was, and had often recourse to it; but I took care to give her a deal of trouble; for whenever I was ordered in my turn to read the Bible, I always selected such chapters as I thought militated against Arians, Socinians etc, and such verses as I deemed favourable to the doctrine of original sin, justification by faith, imputed righteousness, the doctrine of the Trinity etc. On such parts I always placed a particular emphasis, which puzzled and teased the old lady a good deal. . . .

Hitherto I had not frequented the Methodist meetings by the consent or knowledge of my master and mistress; nor had my zeal been so great as to make me openly violate their commands. But as my zeal increased much faster than my knowledge, I soon disregarded their orders, and without hesitation ran away to hear a methodistical sermon as often as I could find an opportunity. One Sunday morning, at eight o'clock my mistress seeing her sons off, and knowing that they were gone to a Methodist meeting, determined to prevent me from doing the same by locking the door, which she accordingly did; on which, in a superstitious mood, I opened the Bible for direction what to do (ignorant Methodists often practise the same superstitious method), and the first words I read were these, "He had given his angels charge concerning thee, lest at any time thou dash thy foot against a stone." This was enough for me; so without a moment's hesitation, I ran up two pairs of stairs to my own room, and out of the window I leaped, to the great terror of my poor mistress. I got up immediately, and ran about two or three hundred yards towards the meeting house; but alas! I could run no farther, my feet and ankles were most intolerably bruised, so that I was obliged to be carried back and put to bed; and it was more than a month before I recovered the use of my limbs. I was ignorant enough to think that the Lord had not used me very well, and resolved not to put so much trust in him for the future. . . .

Memoirs of the First Forty-five Years of the Life of James Lackington, Bookseller, written by himself, in forty-seven letters to a friend, 1791.

Charlotte Charke

My next flight was gardening, a very pleasing and healthful exercise, in which I passed the most part of my time every day. I thought it always proper to imitate the actions of those persons whose characters I chose to represent, and indeed was as changeable as Proteus.

When I had blended the groom and gardener, I conceived, after having worked two or three hours in the morning, a broiled rasher of bacon upon a luncheon of bread in one hand, and a pruning-knife in the other (walking instead of sitting to this elegant meal), making seeds and plants the general subject of my discourse, was the true characteristic of the gardener; as, at other times, a halter and horse-cloth brought into the house, and awkwardly thrown down on a chair, were emblems of my stable profession; with now and then a shrug of the shoulders and a scratch of the head, with a hasty demand for small-beer, and a "God bless you, make haste; I have not a single horse dressed or watered, and here 'tis almost eight o'clock, the poor cattle will think I have forgot 'em; and tomorrow they go a journey, I am sure I'd need take care of 'em." Perhaps this great journey was an afternoon's jaunt to Windsor, within seven miles of our house; however, it served me to give myself as many airs, as if it had been a progress of five hundred miles.

It luckily happened for me that my father was gone to France, and the servant who was in the capacity of groom and gardener, having the misfortune one afternoon to be violently inebriated, took it in his head to abuse the rest of his fellow-servants, which my mother hearing, interfered, and shared equally the insolence of his opprobrious tongue; upon which, at a minute's warning, he was dismissed, to the inexpressible transport, my gentle reader, of your humble servant, having then the full possession of the garden and stables. . . .

One day, upon my mother's paying me a visit in the garden, and approving something I had done there, I rested on my spade, and, with a significant smile and a nod, asked whether she imagined any of the rest of her children would have done as much at my age? adding, very shrewdly, "Come, come, madam, let me tell you, a pound saved is a pound gained"; then proceeded in my office of digging, in which I was at that time most happily employed, and with double labour pursued, to make the strongest impression I could upon my admiring mother's mind, and convince her of the utility of so industrious a child.

I must not forget to inform the reader that my mother had no extraordinary opinion of the fellow's honesty whom she had turned away; and what confirmed it, was tracing his footsteps under the chamber-windows the night after his dismission, and the neighbours had observed him to have been hovering round the house several hours that very evening.

As we had a considerable quantity of plate, my mother was a good deal alarmed with an apprehension of the man's attempting to break in at midnight, which might render us not only liable to be robbed, but murdered. She communicated her fears to me, who most heroically promised to protect her life, at the utmost hazard of my own. Accordingly I desired all the plate might be gathered up, and had it placed in a large flasket by my bedside. This was no small addition to my happiness, as it gave me an opportunity of raising my reputation as a courageous person, which I was extremely fond of being deemed; and in order to establish that character, I stripped the hall and kitchen of their firearms, which consisted of my own little carbine, a heavy blunderbuss, a muscatoon and two brace of pistols, all of which I had loaded with a couple of bullets each before I went to bed; not with any design, upon my word, to yield to my repose, but absolutely kept awake three long and tedious hours, which were from twelve to three, the time I thought most likely for an invasion.

But no such thing happened, for not a mortal approached, in which I thought myself undone, till a friendly dog, who barked at the moon, gave a happy signal, and I bounced from my repository, with infinite obligations to the cur, and fired out of the window piece after piece, re-charging as fast as possible, till I had consumed about a pound of powder, and a proportionable quantity of shot and balls.

'Tis not to be supposed but that the family was, on my first onset in this singular battle (having nothing to combat but the air) soon alarmed. The frequent reports and violent explosions encouraged my kind prompter to this farce to change his lucky bark into an absolute howl, which strongly corroborated with all that had been thought or said in regard to an attempt upon the house. My trembling mother, who lay half expiring with dreadful imaginations, rang her bell, which summons I instantly obeyed, firmly assuring her that all danger was over, for that I heard the villain decamp on the first firing, which decampment was neither more nor less than the rustling of the trees, occasioned by a windy night, for the fellow was absolutely gone to London the very morning I declared war against him, as was afterwards found.

Notwithstanding I was fully convinced I had nothing to conquer but my unconquerable fondness and resolution to acquire the character of a courageous person, I settled that point with the whole family, in begging them not to be under the least apprehension of danger, urging that my constant firing would be the means of preventing any; and bid them consider that the loss of sleep was not to be put in competition with the hazard of their lives.

This reflection made them perfectly easy, and me entirely happy, as I had an unlimited power, without interruption, once in ten minutes, to waste my ammunition to no purpose; and retiring to my rest, as soon as my stock was exhausted, enjoyed in dreams a second idea of my glorious exploits.

A Narrative of the Life of Mrs Charlotte Charke, youngest daughter of Colley Cibber, Esq., written by herself, 1755.

Joseph Arch

I NOW worked my way back to Barford, and at last found myself once more in the old cottage. I had gained both money and experience, I had travelled over large tracts of my native land, I had been tried as a labourer and had not been found wanting; as a mower, as a hedger and ditcher, I had more than held my own with the best. Wherever I had worked, I had given proof that I was not one of the hopeless, helpless nobodies. I was conscious of increased strength, and vigour of mind and body; I had learned where I stood among my fellow-workers, and consequently I was more than ever determined to carve out an upward path for myself, and be a somebody in the world of working men.

It was early in the forties when I made my way back like a homing pigeon to the old Arch roof-tree. I was now a stalwart young man, nearing the end of my teens, a true chip of the old block. There was nothing of the shamefaced prodigal son about me when I set foot in my native village once more, and returned to my father. I had not been wasting my wages in riotous living, and then been reduced to feed on swine husks because I had not a penny piece left to my bad name. No; it was young Jo Arch the worker, not Jo Arch the wastrel, who tramped home from his travels with money in his pocket, money enough to have bought and paid for a fatted calf on his own account, wherewith to give his father a treat. I had been journeying to and fro on the face of a fine broad bit of English earth, seeking what wages I could earn, what work I could get, and what facts I could devour. I found, I got, I devoured, every morsel which came in my way. I read, marked, learned and inwardly digested, as the prayer book says somewhere, all I could lay my hands or ears or eyes on. At the same time I was taking in a supply of facts which would not be digested—tough facts about the land and the labourer, that accumulated and lay within my mind, heavy as a lump of lead, and hard as a stone. No matter what I did, whether I was working with my hands or my head, that mass of indigestible facts was always in the background, worrying and bothering me. I got no peace; it worried and bothered me more and more as each year went by. . . .

Glad as I was to get back home, the old place did not seem the same without my mother. We missed her badly at every turn. I learned then that the working-man's home is no home at all, if there is not a good housewife within doors. Let his wife be a slattern, and a wilful, careless waster—well, then, before very long, there will be woeful want stepping in, bringing angry words and worse behind, and driving love like smoke up the kitchen chimney; let his home be hugger-mugger, and it is only a man in a thousand that will not step down to the public-house for an hour's comfort and enjoyment after his day's labour is over. Who will cast the first stone at him for doing it? Not I— though neither my father nor I went that way. We put up with inconveniences of all sorts, and tried to get along as best we could, rather than run the risk of having dishonest people about us, plundering right and left when we were safe away in the fields. I worked at hedging and ditching and draining, at fence and hurdle making, at any and every job that would bring in good money; it was all in the week's work, and in the evening I would keep pegging away at my books.

Joseph Arch: the Story of His Life, 1898.

George Whitefield

DURING the time of my being at school, I was very fond of reading plays, and have kept from school for days together to prepare myself for acting them. My master, seeing how mine and my school-fellows' vein run, composed something of this kind for us himself, and caused me to dress myself in girl's clothes (which I had often done) to act a part before the Corporation. The remembrance of this has often covered me with confusion of face, and I hope will do so, even to the end of my life.

And I cannot but here observe with much concern of mind, how this way of training up youth has a natural tendency to debauch the mind, to raise ill passions, and to stuff the memory with things as contrary to the gospel of Jesus Christ as light to darkness, heaven to hell. However, though the first thing I had to repent of was my education in general, yet I must always acknowledge my particular thanks are due to my master, for the great pains he took with me and his other scholars, in teaching us to speak and write correctly.

Before I was fifteen, having, as I thought, made a sufficient progress in the classics, and, at bottom, longing to be set at liberty from the confinement of a school, I one day told my mother, since circumstances would not permit her to give me a university education, more learning I thought would spoil me for a tradesman, and therefore I judged it better not to learn Latin any longer. She at first refused to consent, but my corruptions soon got the better of her good nature. Hereupon for some time I went to learn to write only. But my mother's circumstances being much on the decline, and being tractable that way, I from time to time began to assist her occasionally in the public house, till at length I put on my blue apron and my snuffers, washed mops, cleaned rooms, and in one word became professed and common drawer for nigh a year and an half.

But He who was with David when he was following the sheep big with young was with me even here. For notwithstanding I was thus employed in a common inn, and had sometimes the care of the whole house upon my hands, yet I composed two or three sermons, and dedicated one of them in particular to my elder brother. One time I remember I was much pressed to self-examination, and found myself very unwilling to look into my heart. Frequently I read the Bible when sitting up at night. Seeing the boys go by to school has often cut me to the heart. And a dear youth (now with God) would often come entreating me, when serving at the bar, to go to Oxford. My general answer was, "I wish I could." . . .

Having thus lived with my mother for some considerable time, a young student, who was once my school-fellow, and then a servitor of Pembroke College, Oxford, came to pay my mother a visit. Amongst other conversation, he told her how he had discharged all college expenses that quarter, and received a penny. Upon that my mother immediately cried out, "This will do for my son!" Then turning to me, she said, "Will you go to Oxford, George?" I replied, "With all my heart." Whereupon, having the same friends that this young student had, my mother, without delay, waited on them. They promised their interest to get me a servitor's place in the same college. She then applied to my old master, who much approved of my coming to school again.

An Account of God's Dealings with the Reverend Mr George Whitefield, B.A., late of Pembroke College, Oxford, from his Infancy, to the Time of His entering into Holy Orders. Written by Himself, on board the Elizabeth, *Captain Stephenson, bound from* London *to* Philadelphia, *and sent over by Him to be published for the Benefit of the Orphan-house in Georgia. London,* 1740.

John Aubrey

1634, was entered in his Latin grammar by Mr R. Latimer, rector of Leigh Delamere, a mile's fine walk (on a delicate little horse) who had an easy way of teaching: and every time we asked leave to go forth, we had a Latin word from him which at our return we were to tell him again—which in a little while amounted to a good number of words. 'Twas my unhappiness in half a year to lose this good informer by his death, and afterwards was under several dull ignorant rest-in-house teachers till 1638 (12), at which time I was sent to Blandford School in Dorset (William Sutton, B.D., who was ill-natured). . . .

Here I recovered my health, and got my Latin and Greek, the best of any of my contemporaries. The usher had (by chance) a Cowper's Dictionary, which I had never seen before. I was then in Terence. Perceiving his method, I read all in the book where Terence was, and then Cicero—which was the way by which I got my Latin. 'Twas a wonderful help to my fancy, my reading of Ovid's *Metamorphy* in English by Sandys, which made me understand the Latin better. Also, I met accidentally a book of my mother's, Lord Bacon's *Essays,* which first opened my understanding as to morals (for Tully's *Offices* was too crabbed for my young years) and the excellence of the style, or hints and transitions.

I was always enquiring of my grandfather of the old time, the rood-loft, etc., ceremonies, of the priory etc. At 8, I was a kind of engineer, and I fell then to drawing, beginning first with plain outlines, e.g. in drafts of curtains. Then at 9 to colours, having nobody to instruct me; copied pictures in the parlour in a table book. . . .

I was wont (I remember) much to lament with myself that I lived not in a city, e.g. Bristol, where I might have access to watchmakers, locksmiths, etc. I did not very much care for grammar. I had apprehension enough, but my memory not tenacious. So that then was a promising morn enough of an inventive and philosophical head. I had a musical head, inventive, wrote blank verse, had a strong and early impulse to antiquity (strong impulse to Saturn). My wit was always working, but not adroit for verse. I was exceeding mild of spirit; mightily susceptible of fascination. My idea very clear; fancy like a mirror, pure crystal water which the least wind does disorder and unsmooth— so noise or etc. would. . . .

1642, May 2nd, I went to Oxford.

Peace.

Looked through Logic and some Ethics.

1642, *Religio Medici* printed, which first opened my understanding, which I carried to Easton, with Sir Kenelm Digby.

But now Bellona thundered, and as a clear sky is sometimes suddenly overstretched with a dismal cloud and thunder, so was this serene peace by the civil wars through the factions of those times; *vide* Homer's *Odyssey*.

In August following, my father sent for me home, for fear.

In February following, with much ado I got my father to let me to beloved Oxon again, then a garrison *pro rege*. . . .

In April I fell sick of the small-pox at Trinity College; and when I recovered, after Trinity week, my father sent for me into the country again; where I conversed with none but servants and rustics and soldiers quartered, to my great grief (*Odi prophanum vulgus et arceo*), for in those days fathers were not acquainted with their children. It was a most sad life to me, in the prime of my youth, not to have the benefit of an ingenious conversation and scarce any good books—almost a consumption. This sad life I did lead in the country till 1646, at which time I got (with much ado) leave of my father to let me go to the Middle Temple, April the 6th 1646.

24 June following, Oxon was surrendered, and then came to London many of the king's party, with whom I grew acquainted (many of them I knew before). I loved not debauches, but their martial conversation was not so fit for the muses.

November 6, I returned to Trinity College in Oxon again to my great joy; was much made of by the fellows; had their learned conversation, looked on books, music. Here and at Middle Temple (off and on) I (for the most part) enjoyed the greatest felicity of my life (ingenious youths, as rosebuds, imbibe the morning dew) till Dec. 1648 (Christmas Eve's eve) I was sent from Oxon home again to my sick father, who never recovered. Where I was engaged to look after his country business and solicit a law-suit. . . .

Brief Lives, chiefly of contemporaries, set down by
John Aubrey between the years 1669 and 1696.

Mark Pattison

I WAS trying with all my might to become like the men with whom I lived, and affected their phrases before I could honestly use them as being the expression of my real thoughts. I was trying to suppress that which was, all the time, my real self, and to put on the new man—the type by which I was surrounded. The assimilating process, which was not wholly bad, was carried to a certain point, and there arrested, as I shall try to tell in the sequel; and that is the history of my life, and its only interest, so far as it has any.

It was indeed quite necessary for the common conduct of myself that I should become more like others, and take on something of the current fashion, and something of the ordinary motive. I stood sorely in need of this discipline. At the same time the process, necessary as I see it was, had a baneful influence upon character. I was making a constant effort to appear to be, and thus a habit of acting a part, and considering how I looked in it, grew up in me. It was bad enough that I was always surrendering or crushing out my natural judgment in favour of other men's judgment, but it was worse that I was trying to pass myself off for something I was not. For it was of course that my endeavour, from being an endeavour to seem *something* I was not, should slide into an endeavour to seem something *better* than what I was. This gave my whole behaviour an insincerity and affectation which, when discovered, extremely displeased myself, but which I found it impossible to shake off, as it was bound up with the attempt to do and think as others do —an attempt which at that time was indispensable to my existence as a member of society. . . . This constant personation, and considering how I looked in others' eyes, clung about me till very late in life. Had I been thrown more into an active profession I should have rubbed it off sooner, but living a student's life, and only emerging into the sunlight at intervals, this nervous self-consciousness adhered to me long. When at last got rid of, it gave way, not to the ordinary social friction, but to the substantial development of the real self, which had been all the while dormant within me, as I shall relate.

Meanwhile, and at my *début,* this sheepishness, and wondering what others were thinking of me, was a source of unspeakable misery to me. I did not know where to put my hands, how to look, how to carry myself. I tried in vain to find out by what secret other men moved about so unembarrassed. I remember as if it were yesterday the first time I met the Provost (of Oriel) in the street. When I became aware that he was coming I was seized with such a tremor, that in the thought of how I ought to perform my first act of "capping", I omitted the ceremony altogether, and passed him in blank confusion. I saw he knew me and smiled, and I tortured myself with conjecture as to what the smile meant—contempt or compassion. A few days afterwards I met him and Mrs Hawkins again in the back lane; he knew me—he knew us all by sight—and good-naturedly supposing that on the previous occasion I had not recognised him, he advanced towards me, holding out his hand, "Good morning, Mr Pattison." I was again in a state of nervous collapse, but having prepared myself in imagination for the terrible ordeal, I executed according to the rules "ad justum intervallum caput aperiendo", but took no notice of the outstretched and ungloved hand proffered me. I remember now the grunt of dissatisfaction which escaped from the Provost as I tore past, discovering my blunder when it was too late to repair it. I think the Provost's aversion for me dated from this gross exhibition of *maladresse*; and I am not at all surprised at it. He, however, included me in his freshman's dinner-party the very first term. I went like a victim, and sat the allotted two hours in misery. At ringing of chapel-bell we were dismissed, and this time I managed to execute the *nunc dimittis* handshake; rushed to my room, tore off my white choker and my blue swallow-tail coat, with gilt flat buttons, and felt myself again.

Memoirs, 1885.

Anthony Trollope

I GOT into my place without any examining. Looking back now, I think I can see with accuracy what was then the condition of my own mind and intelligence. Of things to be learned by lessons,

I knew almost less than could be supposed possible after the amount of schooling I had received. I could read neither French, Latin, nor Greek. I could speak no foreign language—and I may as well say here as elsewhere that I never acquired the power of really talking French. I have been able to order my dinner and take a railway ticket, but never got much beyond that. Of the merest rudiments of the sciences I was completely ignorant. My handwriting was in truth wretched. My spelling was imperfect. There was no subject as to which examination would have been possible on which I could have gone through an examination otherwise than disgracefully. And yet I think I knew more than the average of young men of the same rank who began life at nineteen. I could have given a fuller list of the names of the poets of all countries, with their subjects and periods—and probably of historians—than many others; and had, perhaps, a more accurate idea of the manner in which my country was governed. I knew the names of all the Bishops, all the Judges, all the Heads of Colleges, and all the Cabinet Ministers—not a very useful knowledge, indeed, but one that had not been acquired without other matter that was more useful. I had read Shakespeare and Byron and Scott, and could talk about them. I had already made up my mind that *Pride and Prejudice* was the best novel in the English language;—a palm which I only partially withdrew after a second reading of *Ivanhoe,* and did not completely bestow elsewhere till *Esmond* was written. And though I would occasionally break down in my spelling, I could write a letter. If I had a thing to say, I could so say it in written words that the readers should know what I meant,—a power which is by no means at the command of all those who come out from these competitive examinations with triumph. Early in life, at the age of fifteen, I had commenced the dangerous habit of keeping a journal, and this I maintained for ten years. The volumes remained in my possession unregarded—never looked at—till 1870, when I examined them and, with many blushes, destroyed them. They convicted me of folly, ignorance, indiscretion, idleness, extravagance, and conceit. But they had habituated me to the rapid use of pen and ink, and taught me how to express myself with facility.

I will mention here another habit which had grown upon me from still earlier years—which I myself often regarded with dismay when I thought of the hours devoted to it, but which, I suppose, must have tended to make me what I have been. As a boy, even as a child, I was thrown much upon myself. I have explained, when speaking of my schooldays, how it came to pass that other boys would not play with me. I was therefore alone, and had to form my plays within myself. Play of some kind was necessary to me, as it has always been. Study was not my bent, and I could not please myself by being all idle. Thus it came to pass that I was always going about with some castle in the air firmly built within my mind. Nor were these efforts in architecture spasmodic, or subject to constant changes from day to day. For weeks, for months, if I remember rightly, from year to year, I would carry on the same tale, binding myself down to certain laws, to certain proportions, and proprieties, and unities. Nothing impossible was ever introduced,—not even anything which, from outward circumstances, would seem to be wildly improbable. I myself was of course my own hero. Such is a necessity of castle-building. But I never became a king, or a duke,—much less, when my height and personal appearance were fixed, could I be an Antinous or six feet high. I never was a learned man, nor even a philosopher. But I was a very clever person, and beautiful young women used to be fond of me. And I strove to be kind of heart, and open of hand, and noble in thought, despising mean things; and altogether I was a very much better fellow than I have ever succeeded in being since. This had been the occupation of my life for six or seven years before I went to the Post Office, and was by no means abandoned, when I commenced my work. There can, I imagine, hardly be a more dangerous mental practice; but I have often doubted whether, had it not been my practice, I should ever have written a novel. I learned in this way to maintain an interest in a fictitious story, to dwell on a work created by my own imagination, and to live in a world altogether outside the world of my own material life. In after years I have done the same,—with this difference, that I have discarded the hero of my early dream, and have been able to lay my own identity aside.

An Autobiography, 1883.

Herbert Spencer

I WAS in boyhood extremely prone to castle-building—a habit which continued throughout youth and into mature life: finally passing, I suppose, into the dwelling on schemes more or less practicable. In early days the habit was such that on going to bed, it was a source of satisfaction to me to think I should be able to lie for a length of time and dwell on the fancies which at the time occupied me; and frequently next morning, on waking, I was vexed with myself because I had gone to sleep before I had revelled in my imagination as much as I had intended.

Often these dreams, becoming literally day-dreams, quite filled my consciousness when waking. Even in the streets my state of abstraction was such that I occasionally talked aloud as I went along; a fact of which I was from time to time made aware by people who turned to look at me. But the strangest instance exhibiting such absorption was this. I had been sent into the town on some commission; got as usual into a train of imaginary adventures; walked through the main streets and suburbs into the country on the other side of the town; eventually came to myself and remembered what I had been sent out for; turned round and walked back again through the town; and arrived at the door of our house before again coming to myself and recollecting my errand.

I believe it is a general belief that castle-building is detrimental;

but I am by no means sure that this is so. In moderation I regard it as beneficial. It is a play of the constructive imagination, and without constructive imagination there can be no high achievement. I believe that the love I then had for it arose from the spontaneous activity of powers which in future life became instrumental to higher things. And here let me remark in passing an accompanying trait. The tendency to absorption above illustrated was, I suspect, a part cause of a peculiarity with which my father often reproached me in the words—"As usual, Herbert, thinking only of one thing at a time." This liability to become so engrossed in one subject, or aspect of a subject, as to quite forget others, led in after-life to sundry disasters.

An Autobiography, 1904.

R. G. Collingwood

My father had plenty of books, and allowed me to read in them as I pleased. Among others, he had kept the books of classical scholarship, ancient history, and philosophy which he had used at Oxford. As a rule I left these alone; but one day when I was eight years old curiosity moved me to take down a little black book lettered on its spine "Kant's Theory of Ethics". It was Abbott's translation of the *Grundlegung zur Metaphysik der Sitten*; and as I began reading it, my small form wedged between the bookcase and the table, I was attacked by a strange succession of emotions. First came an intense excitement. I felt that things of the highest importance were being said about matters of the utmost urgency; things which at all costs I must understand. Then, with a wave of indignation, came the discovery that I could not understand them. Disgraceful to confess, here was a book whose words were English and whose sentences were grammatical, but whose meaning baffled me. Then, third and last, came the strangest emotion of all. I felt that the contents of this book, although I could not understand it, were somehow my business: a matter personal to myself, or rather to some future self of my own. It was not like the common boyish intention to "be an engine-driver when I grow up", for there was no desire in it; I did not, in any natural sense of the word, "want" to master the Kantian ethics when I should be old enough; but I felt as if a veil had been lifted and my destiny revealed.

There came upon me by degrees, after this, a sense of being burdened with a task whose nature I could not define except by saying, "I must think." What I was to think about I did not know; and when, obeying this command, I fell silent and absent-minded in company, or sought solitude in order to think without interruption, I could not have said, and still cannot say, what it was that I actually thought. There were no particular questions that I asked myself; there were no special objects upon which I directed my mind; there was only a formless and aimless intellectual disturbance, as if I were wrestling with a fog.

I know now that this is what always happens when I am in the early stages of work on a problem. Until the problem has gone a long way towards being solved, I do not know what it is; all I an conscious of is this vague perturbation of mind, this sense of being worried about I cannot say what. I know now that the problems of my life's work were taking, deep down inside me, their first embryonic shape. But any one who observed me must have though, as my elders did think, that I had fallen into a habit of loafing, and lost the alertness and quickness of wit that had been so noticeable in my early childhood. My only defence against this opinion, since I did not know and therefore could not explain what was happening to me, was to cover these fits of abstraction with some bodily activity, trifling enough not to distract my attention from my inward wrestling. I was a neat-fingered boy, skilful at making all sorts of things; active in walking, bicycling, or rowing, and throughly practised in sailing a boat. So when the fit was upon me I would set myself to make something quite uninteresting, like a regiment of paper men, or wander aimlessly in the woods or on the mountains, or sail all day in a dead calm. It was painful to be laughed at for playing with paper men; but the alternative, to explain why I did it, was impossible.

An Autobiography, 1939.

Self-Scrutinisers

---◎---

ABRAHAM COWLEY

THOMAS BROWNE

ROBERT GREENE

LORD BYRON

EDWARD GIBBON

DUDLEY RYDER

ELIZABETH FRY

BEATRICE WEBB

THOMAS GRAY

HORACE WALPOLE

WILLIAM WORDSWORTH

RICHARD BAXTER

LESLIE STEPHEN

CHARLES DARWIN

H. G. WELLS

G. K. CHESTERTON

DAVID HUME

JOHN WESLEY

Abraham Cowley

It is a hard and nice subject for a man to write of himself, it grates his own heart to say anything of disparagement, and the reader's ears to hear anything of praise from him. There is no danger from me of offending him in this kind; neither my mind, nor my body, nor my fortune, allow me any materials for that vanity. It is sufficient, for my own contentment, that they preserved me from being scandalous, or remarkable on the defective side. . . . As far as my memory can return back into my past life, before I knew or was capable of guessing what the world, or glories, or business of it were, the natural affections of my soul gave me a secret bent of aversion from them, as some plants are said to turn away from others, by an antipathy imperceptible to themselves, and inscrutable to man's understanding.

On My Self: *Essays,* 1668.

Sir Thomas Browne

Now for that other virtue of charity, without which faith is a mere notion and of no existence, I have ever endeavoured to nourish the merciful disposition and humane inclination I borrowed from my parents, and to regulate it to the written and prescribed laws of charity; and if I hold the true anatomy of myself, I am delineated and naturally framed to such a piece of virtue; for I am of a constitution so general, that it consorts and sympathizeth with all things; I have no antipathy, or rather idiosyncrasy, in diet, humour, air, anything. I wonder not at the French for their dishes of frogs, snails and toadstools, nor at the Jews for locusts and grass-hoppers, but being among them, make them my common viands; and I find they agree with my stomach as well as theirs; I could digest a salad gathered in a churchyard as well as in a garden. I cannot start at the presence of a serpent, scorpion, lizard or salamander; at the sight of a toad or viper, I feel in me no desire to take up a stone to destroy them. I find not in myself those common antipathies that I can discover in others. Those natural repugnances do not touch me, nor do I behold with prejudice the French, Italian, Spaniard or Dutch; but where I find their actions in balance with my countrymen's, I honour, love and embrace them in the same degree. I was born in the eighth climate, but seem to be framed and constellated unto all; I am no plant that will not prosper out of a garden. All places, all airs, make unto me one country; I am in England everywhere, and under any meridian. I have been shipwrecked, yet am not enemy with the sea or winds; I can study, play or sleep in a tempest. In brief, I am averse from nothing, neither plant, animal nor spirit: my conscience would give me the lie if I should say I absolutely detest or hate any essence but the Devil, or so at least abhor anything, but that we might come to composition. If there be any among those common objects of hatred which I can safely say I do contemn and laugh at, it is that great enemy of reason, virtue and religion, the multitude, that numerous piece of monstrosity, which taken asunder seem men, and the reasonable creatures of God; but confused together, make but one great beast, and a monstrosity more prodigious than Hydra; it is no breach of charity to call these fools, it is the style all holy writers have afforded them, set down by Solomon in canonical Scripture, and a point of our faith to believe so.

Religio Medici, 1643.

Robert Greene

I NEED not make long discourse of my parents, who for their gravity and honest life is well known and esteemed among their neighbours, namely in the city of Norwich, where I was bred and born. But as out of one self-same clod of clay there sprouts both stinking weeds and delightful flowers, so from honest parents often grow most dishonest children; for my father had care to have me in my nonage brought up at school, that I might through the study of good letters grow to be a friend to myself, a profitable member to the commonwealth, and a comfort to him in his age. But as early pricks the tree that will prove a thorn, so even in my first years I began to follow that filthiness of mine own desires, and neither to listen to the wholesome admonishment of my parents, nor be ruled by the careful correction of my master. For being at the University of Cambridge, I lighted among wags as lewd as myself, with whom I consumed the flower of my youth, who drew me to travel into Italy and Spain, in which places I saw and practised such villainy as is abominable to declare. Thus by their counsel I sought to furnish myself with coin, which I procured by cunning sleights from my Father and my friends, and my Mother pampered me so long, and secretly helped me to the oil of angels, that I grew thereby prone to all mischiefs; so that being then conversant with notable braggarts, boon companions and ordinary spendthrifts, that practised sundry superficial studies, I became as a scion grafted into the same stock, whereby I did absolutely participate of their nature and qualities.

At my return to England, I ruffled out in my silks, in the habit of Malcontent, and seemed so discontent that no place would please me to abide in, nor no vocation cause me to stay myself in;

but after I had by degrees proceeded Master of Arts, I left the University and away to London, where (after I had continued some short time, and driven myself out of credit with sundry of my friends) I became an author of plays and a penner of love pamphlets, so that I soon grew famous in that quality, that who for that trade gown so ordinary about London as Robin Greene. Young yet in years, though old in wickedness, I began to resolve that there was nothing bad, that was profitable: whereupon I grew so rooted in all mischief that I had as great a delight in wickedness as sundry hath in godliness, and as much felicity I took in villainy as others had in honesty. . . .

Thus my misdemeanours (too many to be recited) caused the most part so much to despise me that in the end I became friendless, except it were in a few alehouses, who commonly for my inordinate expenses would make much of me, until I were on the score, far more than ever I meant to pay by twenty nobles thick. After I had wholly betaken me to the penning of plays (which was my continual exercise) I was so far from calling upon God that I seldom thought on God, but took such delight in swearing and blaspheming the name of God, that none could think otherwise of me, than that I was the child of perdition.

Those vanities and other trifling pamphlets I penned of love and vain fantasies was my chiefest stay of living, and for those my vain discourses I was beloved of the more vainer sort of people, who being my continual companions came still to my lodging, and there would continue quaffing, carousing and surfeiting with me all the day long.

But I thank God that he put it in my head to lay open the most horrible cozenages of the common coney-catchers, cozeners and cross-biters, which I have indifferently handled in those my several discourses already imprinted. And my trust is that those discourses will do great good and be very beneficial to the Commonwealth of England.

But oh my dear wife, whose company and sight I have refrained these six years, I ask God and thee forgiveness for so greatly wronging thee, of whom I seldom or never thought, until now. Pardon me (I pray thee) wheresoever thou art, and God forgive me all my offences.

The Repentance of Robert Greene, Master of Arts, 1592.

Lord Byron

IF this had been begun ten years ago, and faithfully kept !!!—heigho! there are too many things I wish never to have remembered, as it is. Well,—I have had my share of what are called the pleasures of this life, and have seen more of the European and Asiatic world than I have made good use of. They say, "Virtue is its own reward",—it certainly should be paid well for its trouble. At five-and-twenty, when the better part of life is over, one should be *something*;—and what am I? nothing but five -and-twenty and the odd months. What have I seen? the same man all over the world—ay, and woman too. Give me a Mussulman who never asks questions, and a she of the same race who saves one the trouble of putting them. But for this same plague—yellow fever—and Newstead delay, I should have been by this time a second time close to the Euxine. If I can overcome the last, I don't so much mind your pestilence; and at any rate, the spring shall see me there—provided I neither marry myself nor un-marry any one else in the interval. I wish one was—I don't know what I wish. It is odd I never set myself seriously to wishing without attaining it—and repenting. I begin to believe with the good old Magi, that one should only pray for the nation, and not for the individual;—but, on my principle, this would not be very patriotic.

Journal, November 14th, 1813.

Edward Gibbon

THIS was my birthday, on which I entered into the 26th year of my age. This gave me occasion to look a little into myself, and consider impartially my good and bad qualities. It appeared to me, upon this enquiry, that my character was virtuous, incapable of a base action, and formed for generous ones; but that it was proud, violent, and disagreeable in society. These qualities I must endeavour to cultivate, extirpate, or restrain, according to their different tendency. Wit I have none. My imagination is rather strong than pleasing. My memory both capacious and retentive. The shining qualities of my understanding are extensiveness and penetration; but I want both quickness and exactness. As to my situation in life, tho' I may sometimes repine at it, it perhaps is the best adapted to my character. I can command all the conveniences of life, and I can command too that independence, (that first earthly blessing), which is hardly to be met with in a higher or lower fortune. When I talk of my situation, I must exclude that temporary one, of being in the Militia. Tho' I go thro' it with spirit and application, it is both unfit for, and unworthy of me.

Journal, May 8th, 1703.

Dudley Ryder

WENT to Hackney on horseback. Walked the horse all the way. I had a mind to think as I went along, but did not much. It is a strange thing how vanity and love of being observed and esteemed mixes itself insensibly in our most ordinary actions. I could not help as I went along pleasing myself in hopes somebody or other that knew me would meet me in that thinking studious posture. It might give them a notion of me as a great thinker, that knows how to employ myself alone and take pleasure in retirement. This is not the only time I have had that thought in my head, and it has made me put on a more fixed countenance than ordinary.

When I came to Hackney my mother's house was almost filled with ladies. Some of the company stayed with us all night, and I was obliged to spend my time chiefly with them. I had the assurance to put on a certain air of familiarity and indifference towards them which I thought became me very well.

Diary, April 6th, 1716.

Elizabeth Fry

I HAVE many great faults, but I have some dispositions which I should be most thankful for. I believe I feel much for my fellow-creatures; though I think I mostly see into the minds of those I associate with, and am apt to satirise their weaknesses; yet I don't remember ever being any time with one who was not extremely disgusting, but I felt a sort of love for them, and I do hope I would sacrifice my life for the good of mankind. My mind is too much like a looking-glass—objects of all kinds are easily reflected in it, whilst present, but when they go, their reflection is gone also. I have a faint idea of many things, a strong idea of a few; therefore my mind is cultivated badly. I have many straggling, but not many connected ideas. I have the material to form good in my mind, but I am not a sufficiently good artificer to unite them properly together, and make a good consistence; for in some parts I am too hard, in others too soft. I hope and believe the great Artificer is now at work, that if I join my power with the only One who is able to conduct me aright, I may one day be better than I am.

Diary, October 12th, 1798.

Beatrice Webb

THOROUGHLY enjoyed the last month. Have got statistical outline of dock labour for Tower Hamlets.

Certainly, enquiry into social facts is interesting work; but it needs the devotion of a life to do it thoroughly. I feel that the little bit of work I do will be very superficial, and that, until I can take to enquiry as a life-work, and not only as a holiday task, I shall do very little good with it. But I need much preparation. A general but thorough knowledge of English history and literature: a skeleton, the flesh and blood of which I could at any moment gain by specialised study. A theoretical grasp of the growth of industry, and of the present state of industrial organisation. Then the thinking out of principles—of the limits to the subject-matter and the question of method. This, and a good deal more, I need before I am fully prepared for direct observation. A study of this kind is compatible with my home life, with its uniform duty of tender devotedness. Perhaps I shall be free before I am fit for freedom! Even now, my freedom is considerable; more considerable than I have enjoyed since mother's death. Four months of the year I shall be able to devote to actual observation, and if I take my rest in the country, that will not leave much more than six months to be spent in literary preparation of the material collected. But as the observation will necessarily be disjointed and incomplete, it will serve more to clear my own ideas than to form definite pictures of life. My education is yet to come.

In the meantime I am enjoying my life. I see more reason for believing that the sacrifices I have made to a special intellectual desire were warranted by a certain amount of faculty. As yet I have had no proof of this; my capacity has not yet been stamped as current coin; the metal is still soft, and I know not whether it will bear the right impression. Still, I feel power, I feel capacity, even when I discern clearly my own limitations. . . . And the old faith in individual work is returning—in the sanctity of moral and intellectual conviction.

My Apprenticeship, 1926.
Excerpt from her diary, March 3rd, 1887.

Thomas Gray

I KNOW not what degree of satisfaction it will give you to be told that we shall set out from hence the 24th of this month, and not stop above a fortnight at any place in our way. This I feel, that you are the principal pleasure I have to hope for in my own country. Try at least to make me imagine myself not indifferent to you; for I must own I have the vanity of desiring to be esteemed by somebody, and would choose that somebody should be one whom I esteem as much as I do you. As I am recommending myself to your love, methinks I ought to send you my picture (for I am no more what I was, some circumstances excepted, which I hope I need not particularize to you); you must add then, to your former idea, two years of age, reasonable quantity of dulness, a great deal of silence, and something that rather resembles, than is, thinking; a confused notion of many strange and fine things that have swum before my eyes for some time, a want of love for general society, indeed an inability to it. On the good side you may add a sensibility for what others feel, and indulgence for their faults or weaknesses, a love of truth, and detestation of every thing else. Then you have to deduct a little impertinence, a little laughter, a great deal of pride, and some spirits. These are all the alterations I know of, you perhaps may find more. Think not that I have been obliged for this reformation of manners to reason or reflection, but to a severer schoolmistress, Experience. One has little merit in learning her lessons, for one cannot well help it; but they are more useful than others, and imprint themselves in the very heart.

A letter to Richard West, written from Florence, April 21st, 1741.

Horace Walpole

HERE I am, at Houghton! and alone in this spot, where (except two hours last month) I have not been in sixteen years! Think, what a crowd of reflections!—No, Gray and forty church-yards could not furnish so many. Nay, I know one must feel them with greater indifference than I possess, to have the patience to put them into verse. Here I am, probably for the last time of my life, though not for the last time—every clock that strikes tells me I am an hour nearer to yonder church—that church, into which I have not yet had courage to enter, where lies that mother on whom I doted, and who doted on me! There are the two rival mistresses of Houghton, neither of whom ever wished to enjoy it! There too lies he who founded its greatness, to contribute to whose fall Europe was embroiled—there he sleeps in quiet and dignity, while his friend and his foe, rather his false ally and real enemy, Newcastle and Bath, are exhausting the dregs of their pitiful lives in squabbles and pamphlets!

The surprise the pictures give me is again renewed—accustomed for many years to see nothing but wretched daubs and varnished copies at auctions, I look at these as enchantment. My own description of them seems poor—but shall I tell you truly—the majesty of Italian ideas almost sinks before the warm nature of Flemish colouring! Alas! Don't I grow old? My young imagination was fired with Guido's ideas—must they be plump and prominent as Abishag to warm me now? Does great youth feel with poetic limbs, as well as see with poetic eyes? In one respect I am very young; I cannot satiate myself with looking—an incident contributed to make me feel this more strongly. A party arrived, just as I did, to see the house, a man and three women in riding-dresses, and they rode post through the apartments—I could not hurry before them fast enough—they were not so long in *seeing* for the first time, as I could have been in one room to examine what I knew by heart. I remember formerly being often diverted with this kind of *seers*—they come, ask what such a room is called, in which Sir Robert lay, write it down, admire a lobster or a cabbage in a market-piece, dispute whether the last room was green or purple, and then hurry to the inn for fear the fish should be overdressed—how different my sensations! Not a picture here, but recalls a history; not one, but I remember in Downing Street or Chelsea, where queens and crowds admired them, though *seeing* them as little as these travellers!

When I had drunk tea, I strolled into the garden—they told me, it was now called *the pleasure ground*—what a dissonant idea of pleasure—those groves, those *alleés,* where I have passed so many charming moments, are now stripped up, or overgrown;

many fond paths I could not unravel, though with a very exact clue in my memory—I met two gamekeepers, and a thousand hares! In the days when all my soul was tuned to pleasure and vivacity (and you will think perhaps it is far from being out of tune yet) I hated Houghton and its solitude—yet I loved this garden; as now, with many regrets, I love Houghton—Houghton, I know not what to call it, a monument of grandeur or ruin! . . .

A letter to George Montagu, March 25th, 1761.

William Wordsworth

And so I dare to hope,
Though changed, no doubt, from what I was when first
I came among these hills; when like a roe
I bounded o'er the mountains, by the sides
Of the deep rivers, and the lonely streams,
Wherever nature led: more like a man
Flying from something that he dreads than one
Who sought the thing he loved. For nature then
(The coarser pleasures of my boyish days,
And their glad animal movements all gone by)
To me was all in all. I cannot paint
What then I was. The sounding cataract
Haunted me like a passion: the tall rock,
The mountain, and the deep and gloomy wood,
Their colours and their forms, were then to me
An appetite; a feeling and a love,
That had no need of a remoter charm,
By thought supplied, nor any interest
Unborrowed from the eye. That time is past,
And all its aching joys are now no more,
And all its dizzy raptures. Not for this

Faint I, nor mourn nor murmur; other gifts
Have followed; for such loss, I would believe,
Abundant recompense. For I have learned
To look on nature, not as in the hour
Of thoughtless youth; but hearing oftentimes
The still, sad music of humanity,
Nor harsh nor grating, though of ample power
To chasten and subdue. And I have felt
A presence that disturbs me with the joy
Of elevated thoughts; a sense sublime
Of something far more deeply interfused,
Whose dwelling is the light of setting suns,
And the round ocean and the living air,
And the blue sky, and in the mind of man:
A motion and a spirit, that impels
All thinking things, all objects of all thought,
And rolls through all things. Therefore am I still
A lover of the meadows and the woods
And mountains; and of all that we behold
From this green earth; of all the mighty world
Of eye, and ear, both what they half create,
And what perceive; well pleased to recognise
In nature and the language of the sense
The anchor of my purest thoughts, the nurse,
The guide, the guardian of my heart, and soul
Of all my moral being.

*Lines Composed a Few Miles above Tintern Abbey, on revisiting
the Banks of the Wye during a tour, July 13, 1798.*

Richard Baxter

I WAS once wont to meditate on my own heart, and to dwell at home and look little higher; I was still poring either on my sins and wants, or examining my sincerity; but now, though I am greatly convinced of the need of heart-acquaintance and employment, yet I see more need of a higher work, and that I should look often upon Christ, and God, and heaven, than upon my own heart. At home I can find distempers to trouble me, and some evidences of my peace; but it is above that I must find matter of delight and joy and love and peace itself. Therefore I would have one thought at home upon myself and sins, and many thoughts above upon the high and amiable and beautifying objects.

Heretofore I knew much less than now, and yet was not half so much acquainted with my ignorance. I had a great delight in the daily new discoveries which I made, and of the light which shined in upon me (like a man that cometh into a country where he never was before); but I little knew either how imperfectly I understood those very points whose discovery so much delighted me, or how much might be said against them, nor how many things I was yet a stranger to. But now I find far greater darkness upon all things, and perceive how very little it is that we know in comparison of that which we are ignorant of, and have far meaner thoughts of my own understanding, though I must needs know that it is better furnished than it was then.

Self-Analysis and Life-Review, written about 1660.

Leslie Stephen

MY Cambridge life was cut short by my inability, unfortunate or otherwise, to come to terms with the Thirty-nine Articles. I was not, indeed, cast out by the orthodox indignation of my colleagues. At Cambridge, I have said, there was no bigotry; I was treated with all possible kindness, and for a time continued to reside, and to take some part in college work. But I had to resign my tutorship, which involved specifically clerical functions, and at that time a University career offered few prospects to a layman. A Fellow who was also a clergyman might soar upwards towards the episcopal bench; and I am often tempted to regret that I did not swallow my scruples and aim at some modest ecclesiastical preferment. Bishops indeed have fallen upon evil days; they no longer enjoy the charming repose of the comfortable dignitaries of the eighteenth century. But I should dearly like a deanery. To hold such a position as was held by Milman or Stanley seems to me the very ideal aim for a man of any literary taste; and, what with the broad church and the "higher criticism" of later days, it does not seem that it need have been very hard to follow old Hobbes's advice and swallow your pill without chewing it. However, it was not to be; and I had to accept the only practicable alternative, and exchange the pulpit for the press. I therefore cannot boast that I took to the literary profession from an overflowing love of letters. I had to scribble for the sufficient but not elevated reason that no other honest profession was open to me. Possibly I do not think so highly of the calling as some men whom I envy and admire, because in adopting a literary career they are obeying their spontaneous vocation. A friend, only too partial a friend, lately attributed to me the opinion that on the whole books ought not to be written.

I do not accept that rather sweeping theory as an accurate interpretation of my view. I should have been glad to write some books—a new *Paradise Lost,* for example, or, say, a *Wealth of Nations*—if I had seen my way to such achievements; but I rather doubt whether the familiar condemnation of mediocre poetry should not be extended to mediocrity in every branch of literature. In other walks of life a man may be doing something useful even if his walk be of the humblest. The world is the better, no doubt, even for an honest crossing-sweeper. But I often think that the value of second-rate literature is, not small, but simply zero.

Some Early Impressions, 1903.

Charles Darwin

I AM not conscious of any change in my mind during the last thirty years, excepting in one point presently to be mentioned; nor indeed could any change have been expected unless one of general deterioration. But my father lived to his eighty-third year with his mind as lively as ever it was, and all his faculties undimmed; and I hope that I may die before my mind fails to a sensible extent. I think that I have become a little more skilful in guessing right explanations and in devising experimental tests; but this may probably be the result of mere practice, and of a larger store of knowledge. I have as much difficulty as ever in expressing myself clearly and concisely; and this difficulty has caused me a very great loss of time; but it has had the compensating advantage of forcing me to think long and intently about every sentence, and thus I have been often led to see errors in reasoning and in my own observations or those of others. . . .

I have said that in one respect my mind has changed during the last twenty or thirty years. Up to the age of thirty, or beyond it, poetry of many kinds, such as the works of Milton, Gray,

Byron, Wordsworth, Coleridge, and Shelley, gave me great
pleasure, and even as a schoolboy I took great delight in Shakespeare, especially in the historical plays. I have also said that
formerly pictures gave me considerable, and music very great,
delight. But now for many years I cannot endure to read a line
of poetry: I have tried lately to read Shakespeare, and found it
so intolerably dull that it nauseated me. I have also almost lost
any taste for pictures or music. Music generally sets me thinking
too energetically on what I have been at work on, instead of giving
me pleasure. I retain some taste for fine scenery, but it does not
cause me the exquisite delight which it formerly did. On the
other hand, novels which are a work of the imagination, though
not of a very high order, have been for years a wonderful relief
and pleasure to me, and I often bless all novelists. A surprising
number have been read aloud to me, and I like all if moderately
good, and if they do not end unappily—against which a law ought
to be passed. A novel, according to my taste, does not come into
the first class unless it contains some person who one can
thoroughly love, and if it be a pretty woman, all the better.

This curious and lamentable loss of the higher aesthetic tastes
is all the odder, as books on history, biographies and travels,
(independently of any scientific facts which they may contain),
and essays on all sorts of subjects interest me as much as ever
they did. My mind seems to have become a kind of machine for
grinding general laws out of large collections of facts, but why
this should have caused the atrophy of that part of the brain
alone, on which the higher tastes depend, I cannot conceive.
A man with a mind more highly organised or better constituted
than mine would not, I suppose, thus have suffered; and if I
had to live my life again I would have made it a rule to read some
poetry and listen to some music at least once every week; for
perhaps the parts of my brain now atrophied could thus have
been kept active through use. The loss of these tastes is a loss
of happiness, and may possibly be injurious to the intellect, and
more probably to the moral character, by enfeebling the emotional
part of our nature.

My books have sold largely in England, have been translated into many languages, and passed through several editions in foreign countries. I have heard it said that the success of a work abroad is the best test of its enduring value. I doubt whether this is at all trustworthy; but judged by this standard my name ought to last a few years. Therefore it may be worth while for me to try to analyse the mental qualities and the conditions on which my success has depended; though I am aware that no man can do this correctly.

I have no great quickness of apprehension or wit, which is so remarkable in some clever men, for instance Huxley. I am therefore a poor critic: a paper or book, when first read, generally excites my admiration, and it is only after considerable reflection that I perceive the weak points. My power to follow a long and purely abstract train of thought is very limited; I should, moreover, never have succeeded with metaphysics or mathematics. My memory is extensive, yet hazy; it suffices to make me cautious by vaguely telling me that I have observed or read something opposed to the conclusions which I am drawing, or on the other hand in favour of it; and after a time I can generally recollect where to search for my authority. So poor in one sense is my memory that I have never been able to remember for more than a few days a single date or a line of poetry.

Some of my critics have said, "Oh, he is a good observer, but has no power of reasoning." I do not think that this can be true, for the *Origin of Species* is one long argument from beginning to end, and it has convinced not a few able men. No one could have written it without having some power of reasoning. I have a fair share of invention and common sense or judgment, such as every fairly successful lawyer or doctor must have, but not, I believe, in any higher degree.

On the favourable side of the balance, I think that I am superior to the common run of men in noticing things which easily escape attention, and in observing them carefully. My industry has been nearly as great as it could have been in the observation and collection of facts. What is far more important, my love of natural science has been steady and ardent. This pure love has, however, been much aided by the ambition to be esteemed by my fellow naturalists. From my early youth I have had the strongest desire to understand or explain whatever I observed,—that is, to group all facts under some general laws. These causes combined have given me the patience to reflect or ponder for any number of years over any unexplained problem. As far as I can judge, I am not apt to follow blindly the lead of other men. I have steadily endeavoured to keep my mind free, so as to give up any hypothesis, however much beloved, (and I cannot resist forming one on every subject), as soon as facts are shown to be against it. . . .

My habits are methodical, and this has been of not a little use for my particular line of work. Lastly, I have had ample leisure from not having to earn my own bread. Even ill-health, though it has annihilated several years of my life, has saved me from the distractions of society and amusement.

Therefore, my success as a man of science, whatever this may have amounted to, has been determined, as far as I can judge, by complex and diversified mental qualities and conditions. Of these, the most important have been—the love of science—unbounded patience and long reflecting over any subject—industry in observing and collecting facts—and a fair share of invention as well as of common-sense. With such moderate abilities as I possess, it is truly surprising that thus I should have influenced to a considerable extent the beliefs of scientific men on some important points.

An Autobiography, written 1876.

H. G. Wells

THE brain upon which my experiences have been written is not a particularly good one. If there were brain-shows, as there are cat and dog shows, I doubt if it would even get a third class prize. Upon quite a number of points it would be marked below the average. In a little private school in a small town on the outskirts of London it seemed good enough, and that gave me a helpful conceit about it in early struggles, where confidence was half the battle. It was a precocious brain, so that I was classified with boys older than myself right up to the end of a brief school career which closed before I was fourteen. But compared with the run of brains I meet nowadays, it seems a poorish instrument. I won't even compare it with such cerebra as the full and subtly simple brain of Einstein, the wary, quick and flexible one of Lloyd George, the abundant and rich grey matter of G. B. Shaw, Julian Huxley's store of knowledge or my own eldest son's fine and precise instrument. But in relation to everyday people with no claim to mental distinction I still find it at a disadvantage. The names of places and people, numbers, quantities and dates, for instance, are easily lost or get a little distorted. It snatches at them and often lets them slip again. I cannot do any but the simplest sums in my head, and when I used to play bridge, I found my memory of the consective tricks, and my reasoning about the playing of the cards, inferior to nine out of ten of the people I played with. I lose at chess to almost anyone, and though I have played a spread-out patience called Miss Milligan for the past fifteen years, I have never acquired a sufficient sense of the patterns of 104 cards to make it anything more than a game of chance and feeling. Although I have learnt and relearnt French since my school days, and have lived a large part of each year for the past eight years in France, I have never acquired a flexible diction or a good accent, and I cannot follow French people when they are talking briskly—and they always talk briskly. Such other languages as Spanish, Italian and German I have picked up from a grammar or conversation book sufficiently to serve the purposes of travel, only to lose even that much as soon as I ceased to use them. London is my own particular city; all my life I have been going about in it, and yet the certitude of the taxi-cab driver is a perpetual amazement to me. If I wanted to walk from Hoxton to Chelsea without asking my way, I should have to sit down to puzzle over a map for some time. All this indicates a loose rather inferior mental texture, inexact reception, bad storage and uncertain accessibility. . . . I think my brain has always been very much as it is now, except perhaps for a certain slowing down.

And I believe that its defects are mainly innate. It was not a good brain to begin with, although certain physical defects of mine, and bad early training, may have increased faults that might have been corrected by an observant master. The atmosphere of my home and early upbringing was not a highly educative atmosphere; words were used inexactly, and mispronounced, and so a certain timidity of utterance and a disposition to mumble and avoid doubtful or difficult words and phrases may have worked back into my mental texture. My eyes have different focal lengths, and nobody discovered this until I was over thirty. Columns of figures and lines of print are as a result apt to get a little dislocated, and this made me bad at arithmetic, and blurred my impression of the form of words. It was only about the age of thirteen, when I got away with algebra, Euclid's elements and, a little later, the elements of trigonometry, that I realised I was not a hopeless duffer at mathematics. But here comes an item on the credit side; I found Euclid easy reading, and solved the simple "riders" in my textbook with a facility my schoolmaster found exemplary. I also became conceited about my capacity for "problems" in algebra. And by eleven or twelve, in some way I cannot trace, I had taken to drawing rather vigorously and freshly. . . . I know practically nothing of brain structure, but it seems probable to me that this relative readiness to grasp form and relation indicates that the general shape and arrangement of my brain is better than the quality of its cells, fibres and bloodvessels. I have a quick sense of form and proportion; I have a brain good for outlines. Most of my story will carry out that suggestion.

My perceptions do not seem to be so thorough, vivid and compelling as those of many people I meet, and it is rare that my impressions of things glow. There is a faint element of inattention in all I do; it is as if white was mixed into all the pigments of my life. I am rarely *vivid* to myself. I am just a little slack, not wholly and continuously interested, prone to be indolent and cold-hearted. I am readily bored. When I try to make up for this, I am inevitably a little "forced" when dealing with things, and a little "forced" and "charming" with people. You will find this coming out when I tell of my failure as a draper's assistant and of my relations to my intimate friends. You will discover a great deal of evasion and refusal in my story.

Nature has a way of turning even biological defects into advantages, and I am not sure how far what may be called my success in life has not been due to this undertow of indifference. I have not been easily carried away by immediate things and made to forget the general in the particular. There is a sort of journalistic legend that I am a person of boundless enthusiasm and energy. Nothing could be farther from the reality. For all my desire to be interested, I have to confess that for most things and people I don't care a damn. Writing numbers of books and articles is evidence not of energy but of sedentary habits. People with a real quantitative excess of energy and enthusiasm become Mussolinis, Hitlers, Stalins, Gladstones, Beaverbrooks, Northcliffes, Napoleons. It takes generations to clean up after them. But what I shall leave behind me will not need cleaning up. Just because of that constitutional apathy it will be characteristically free from individual Woosh and it will be available and it will go on for as long as it is needed.

An Experiment in Autobiography, 1934.

G. K. Chesterton

WHAT surprises me in looking back on youth, and even on boyhood, is the extreme rapidity with which it can think its way back to fundamental things. At a very early age I had thought my way back to thought itself. It is a very dreadful thing to do; for it may lead to thinking that there is nothing but thought. At this time I did not distinguish very clearly between dreaming and waking; not only as a mood, but as a metaphysical doubt, I felt as if everything might be a dream. It was as if I had myself projected the universe from within, with all its trees and stars; and that is so near to the notion of being God that it is manifestly even nearer to going mad. Yet I was not mad, in any medical or physical sense; I was simply carrying the scepticism of my time as far as it would go. And I soon found it would go a great deal further than most of the sceptics went. When dull atheists came and explained to me that there was nothing but matter, I listened with a sort of calm horror of detachment, suspecting that there was nothing but mind. I have always felt that there was something thin and third-rate about materialists and materialism ever since. The atheist told me so pompously that he did not believe there was any God; and there were moments when I did not even believe there was any atheist.

As with mental, so with moral extremes. There is something truly menacing in the thought of how quickly I could imagine the maddest, when I had never committed the mildest crime. Something may have been due to the atmosphere of the Decadents, and their perpetual hints of the luxurious horrors of paganism; but I am not disposed to dwell much on that defence; I suspect I manufactured most of my morbidities for myself. But anyhow, it is true that there was a time when I had reached

99

that condition of moral anarchy within, in which a man says, in the words of Wilde, "Atys with the blood-stained knife was better than the thing I am." I have never indeed felt the faintest temptation to the particular madness of Wilde; but I could at this time imagine the worst and wildest disproportions and distortions of more normal passion; the point is that the whole mood was overpowered and oppressed with a sort of corruption of imagination. As Bunyan, in his morbid period, described himself as prompted to utter blasphemies, I had an overpowering impulse to record or draw horrible ideas and images; plunging deeper and deeper as in a blind spiritual suicide. I had never heard of Confession, in any serious sense, in those days; but that is what is really needed in such cases. I fancy they are not uncommon cases. Anyhow, the point is here that I dug quite low enough to discover the devil; and even in some dim way to recognise the devil. At least I never, even in this first vague and sceptical stage, indulged very much in the current arguments about the relativity of evil or the unreality of sin. Perhaps, when I eventually emerged as a sort of theorist, and was described as an Optimist, it was because I was one of the few people in that world of diabolism who really believed in devils.

In truth, the story of what was called my Optimism was rather odd. When I had been for some time in these, the darkest depths of the contemporary pessimism, I had a strong inward impulse to revolt; to dislodge this incubus or throw off this nightmare. But as I was still thinking the thing out by myself, with little help from philosophy and no real help from religion, I invented a rudimentary and makeshift mystical theory of my own. It was substantially this; that even mere existence, reduced to its most primary limits, was extraordinary enough to be exciting. Anything was magnificent as compared with nothing. Even if the very daylight were a dream, it was a day-dream; it was not a nightmare. The mere fact that one could wave one's arms and legs about (or those dubious external features in the landscape which were called one's arms and legs) showed that it had not the mere paralysis of a nightmare. Or if it was a nightmare, it was an enjoyable nightmare. In fact, I had wandered to a position not very far from the phrase of my Puritan grandfather, when he said that he would thank God for his creation if he were a lost soul. I hung on to the remains of religion by one thin thread of thanks.

Autobiography, 1936.

David Hume

THE *intense* view of these manifold contradictions and imperfections in human reason has so wrought upon me, and heated my brain, that I am ready to reject all belief and reasoning, and can look upon no opinion even as more probable or likely than another. Where am I, or what? From what causes do I derive my existence, and to what condition shall I return? Whose favour shall I court, and whose anger must I dread? What beings surround me? and on whom have I any influence, or who have any influence on me? I am confounded with all these questions, and begin to fancy myself in the most deplorable condition imaginable, environed with the deepest darkness and utterly deprived of the use of every member and faculty.

Most fortunately it happens, that since reason is incapable of dispelling these clouds, nature herself suffices to that purpose, and cures me of this philosophical melancholy and delirium, either by relaxing this bent of mind, or by some avocation, and lively impression of my senses, which obliterates all these chimeras. I dine, I play a game of backgammon, I converse, and am merry with my friends, and when after three or four hours' amusement I would return to these speculations, they appear so cold and strained and ridiculous that I cannot find it in my heart to enter into them any farther.

Here then I find myself absolutely and necessarily determined to live and talk and act like other people in the common affairs of life. But notwithstanding that my natural propensity, and the course of my animal spirits and passions reduce me to this indolent belief in the general maxims of the world, I still feel such remains of my former disposition that I am ready to throw all my books and papers into the fire, and resolve never more to renounce the pleasures of life for the sake of reasoning and philosophy. For those are my sentiments in that splenetic humour, which governs me at present. I may, nay I must, yield to the current of nature, in submitting to my senses and understanding; and in this blind submission I show most perfectly my sceptical disposition and principles. But does it follow, that I must strive against the current of nature, which leads me to indolence and pleasure; that I must seclude myself, in some measure, from the commerce and society of men, which is so agreeable; and that I must torture my brain with subtleties and sophistries, at the very time that I cannot satisfy myself concerning the reasonableness of so painful an application, nor have any tolerable prospect of arriving by its means at truth and certainty? Under what obligation do I lie of making such an abuse of time? And to what end can it serve either for the service of mankind, or for my own private interest? No: if I must be a fool, as all those who reason or believe anything *certainly* are, my follies shall at least be natural and agreeable. Where I strive against my inclination, I shall have a good reason for my resistance; and will no more be led a-wandering into such dreary solitudes and rough passages as I have hitherto met with.

These are the sentiments of my spleen and indolence; and indeed I must confess that philosophy has nothing to oppose to them, and expects a victory more from the returns of a serious good-humoured disposition than from the force of reason and conviction. In all the incidents of life we ought still to preserve our scepticism. If we believe that fire warms or water refreshes, 'tis only because it costs us too much pains to think otherwise. Nay, if we are philosophers, it ought only to be upon sceptical principles, and from an inclination which we feel to the employing of ourselves after that manner. Where reason is lively and mixes itself with some propensity, it ought to be assented to. Where it does not, it never can have any title to operate upon us.

At the time, therefore, that I am tired with amusement and company, and have indulged a reverie in my chamber, or a solitary walk by a river-side, I feel my mind all collected within itself, and am naturally *inclined* to carry my view into all those subjects about which I have met so many disputes in the course of my reading and conversation. I cannot forbear having a curiosity to be acquainted with the principles of moral good and evil, the nature and foundation of government, and the cause of those several passions and inclinations which actuate and govern me. I am uneasy to think I approve of one object and disapprove of another, call one thing beautiful and another deformed, decide concerning truth and falsehood, reason and folly, without knowledge upon what principles I proceed. I am concerned for the condition of the learned world, which lies under such a deplorable ignorance in all these particulars. I feel an ambition arise in me of contributing to the instruction of mankind, and of acquiring a name by my inventions and discoveries. These sentiments spring up naturally in my present disposition; and should I endeavour to banish them, by attaching myself to any other business or diversion, I *feel* I should be a loser in point of pleasure; and this is the origin of my philosophy.

A Treatise of Human Nature, 1739.

John Wesley

I THIS day enter on my eighty-fifth year, and what cause have I to praise God, as for a thousand spiritual blessings, so for bodily blessings also! It is true, I am not so agile as I was in time past. I do not run or walk so fast as I did, my sight is a little decayed, my left eye is grown dim, and hardly serves me to read; I have daily some pain in the ball of my right eye, as also in my right temple, (occasioned by a blow received some months since,) and in my right shoulder and arm, which I impute partly to a sprain and partly to the rheumatism. I find likewise some decay in my memory with regard to names and things lately past, but not at all with regard to what I have read or heard twenty, forty or sixty years ago; neither do I find any decay in my hearing, smell, taste or appetite, (though I want but a third part of the food I did once,) nor do I feel any such thing as weariness, either in travelling or preaching, and I am not conscious of any delay in writing sermons, which I do as readily and, I believe, as correctly, as ever. To what cause can I impute this, that I am as I am? First, doubtless, to the power of God fitting me for the work to which I am called, as long as He pleases to continue me therein; and next, subordinately to this, to the prayers of His children. May we not impute it as inferior means, 1. To my constant exercise and change of air? 2. To my never having lost a night's sleep, sick or well, at land or sea, since I was born? 3. To my having sleep at command, so that whenever I feel myself almost worn out, I call it and it comes, day or night? 4. To my having constantly, for above sixty years, risen at four in the morning? 5. To my constant preaching at five in the morning for fifty years? 6. To my having had so little pain in my life, and so little sorrow and anxious care? Even now, though

JOHN WESLEY

I find pain daily in my eye, or temple, or arm, yet it is never violent, and seldom lasts many minutes at a time. Whether or not this is sent to give me warning that I am shortly to quit this tabernacle, I do not know; but be it one way or the other, I have only to say,

> My remnant of days
> I spend in His praise,
>   Who died the whole world to redeem:
> Be they many or few,
> My days are His due,
>   And they all are devoted to Him.

Journal, June 28th, 1788.

Women
In Love

—————❦—————

ELIZABETH BARRETT BROWNING

ANNE HALKETT

ISABEL BURTON

HARRIET MARTINEAU

MARIA NUGENT

DOROTHY OSBORNE

MARY WORTLEY MONTAGU

ANNE FANSHAWE

MARGARET CAVENDISH

Elizabeth Barrett Browning

MY family had been so accustomed to the idea of my living on
and on in that room, that while my heart was eating itself,
their love for me was consoled, and at last the evil grew scarcely
perceptible. It was no want of love in them, and quite natural
in itself; we all get used to the thought of a tomb; and I was
buried, that was the whole. It was a little thing, even for myself,
a short time ago, and really it would be pneumatological curiosity if I could describe and let you see how perfectly, for years
together, after what broke my heart at Torquay, I lived on the
outside of my life, blindly and darkly from day to day, as completely dead to hope of any kind as if I had my face against a
grave, never feeling a personal instinct, taking trains of thought
to carry out as an occupation absolutely indifferent to the *me*
which is in every human being. Nobody quite understood this
of me, because I am not morally a coward, and have a hatred of
all the forms of audible groaning. But God knows what is within,
and how utterly I had abdicated myself and thought it not worth
while to put out my finger to touch my share of life. Even my
poetry, which suddenly grew an interest, was a thing on the
outside of me, a thing to be done, and then done! What people
said of it did not touch *me*. A thoroughly morbid and desolate
state it was, which I look back to now with the sort of horror
with which one would look to one's graveclothes, if one had
been clothed with them by mistake during a trance.

And now I will tell you. It is nearly two years since I have
known Mr Browning. Mr Kenyon wished to bring him to see
me five years ago, as one of the lions of London who roared the
gentlest and was best worth my knowing, but I refused then,
in my blind dislike of seeing strangers. Immediately, however,

after the publication of my last volumes, he wrote to me, and we
had a correspondence which ended in my agreeing to receive
him as I never had received any other man. I did not know why,
but it was utterly impossible for me to refuse to receive him,
though I consented against my will. He writes the most exquisite
letters possible, and has a way of putting things which I have
not, a way of putting aside—so he came. He came, and with our
personal acquaintance began his attachment for me, a sort of
infatuation call it, which resisted the various denials which were
my plain duty at the beginning, and has persisted past them all.
I began with a grave assurance that I was in an exceptional
position and saw him in consequence of it, and that if ever he
recurred to that subject again I could never see him again while
I lived, and he believed me and was silent. To my mind, indeed,
it was a bare impulse—a generous man of quick sympathies
taking up a sudden interest with both hands! So I thought, but
in the meantime the letters and the visits rained down more and
more, and in every one there was something which was too
slight to analyse and notice, but too decided not to be understood; so that at last, when the "proposed respect" of the silence
gave way, it was rather less dangerous. So then I showed him
how he was throwing into the ashes his best affections—how
the common gifts of youth and cheerfulness were behind
me—how I had not the strength, even of *heart*, for the ordinary
duties of life—everything I told him and showed him. "Look at
this—and this—and this", throwing down all my disadvantages.
To which he did not answer by a single compliment, but simply
that he had not then to choose, and that I might be right or that
he might be right, he was not there to decide; but that he loved
me and should to his last hour. He said that the freshness of
youth had passed with him, and that he had studied the world
out of books and seen many women, yet had never loved one
until he had seen me. That he knew himself, and knew that, if
ever so repulsed, he should love me to his last hour—it should be
first and last. At the same time, he would not tease me, he would
wait twenty years if I pleased, and then, if life lasted so long for

both of us, then when it was ending perhaps, I might understand him and feel that I might have trusted him. For my health,
he had believed when he first spoke that I was suffering from an
incurable injury of the spine, and that he could never hope to see
me stand up before his face, and he appealed to my womanly
sense of what a pure attachment should be—whether such a
circumstance, if it had been true, was inconsistent with it. He
preferred, he said, of free and deliberate choice, to be allowed
to sit only an hour a day by my side, to the fulfilment of the
brightest dream which should exclude me, in any possible
world.

I tell you so much, my ever dearest friend, that you may see
the manner of man I have had to do with, and the sort of attachment which for nearly two years has been drawing and winning
me. I know better than any in the world, indeed, what Mr
Kenyon once unconsciously said before me, that "Robert
Browning is great in everything." Then, when you think how
this element of an affection so pure and persistent, cast into my
dreary life, must have acted on it—how little by little I was drawn
into the persuasion that something was left, and that still I
could do something for the happiness of another—and he what
he was, for I have deprived myself of the privilege of praising
him—then it seemed worth while to take up with that unusual
energy (for me!), expended in vain last year, the advice of the
physicians that I should go to a warm climate for the winter. . . .

A letter to Mrs Martin, written at Pisa, October 20th, 1846.

Anne Halkett

BUT finding both by my mother and my Lord Howard that they intended nothing but to part us, so as never to meet again, except it was as strangers, Mr Howard was very importunate to have an opportunity to speak with me that night, which I gave. My sister being only with me, we came down together to the room I appointed to meet with him. I confess I never saw those two passions of love and regret more truly represented, nor could any person express greater affection and resolution of constancy, which with many solemn oaths he sealed, of never loving or marrying any but myself. I was not satisfied with his swearing to future performances, since I said both he and I might find it most convenient to retract; but this I did assure him, as long as he was constant he should never find a change in me, for though duty did oblige me not to marry without my mother's consent, yet it would not tie me to marry without my own.

My sister at this rises, and said, "I did not think you would have engaged me to be a witness to both your resolutions to continue what I expected you'd rather have laid aside, and therefore I will leave you."

"Oh madam," said he, "can you imagine I love at that rate as to have it shaken with any storm? No: were I secure your sister would not suffer in my absence by her mother's severity, I would not care what misery I were exposed to; but to think I should be the occasion of trouble to the person in the earth that I love most is insupportable."

And with that he fell down in a chair that was behind him, but as one without all sense, which I must confess did so much move me that, laying aside all former distance I had kept him at, I sat down upon his knee, and laying my head near his I suffered him to kiss me, which was a liberty I never gave before, nor had not then had I not seen him so overcome with grief; which I endeavoured to suppress with all the encouragement I could, but still pressing him to be obedient to his father, either in going abroad or staying at home, as he thought most convenient.

"No," said he, "since they will not allow me to converse with you, France will be more agreeable to me than England, nor will I go there except I have liberty to come here again and take my leave of you."

To that I could not disagree if they thought fit to allow it; and so my sister and I left him, but she durst not own to my mother where she had been.

The Autobiography of Lady Halkett.

Isabel Burton

THEY say it is time I married (perhaps it is); but it is never time to marry any man one does not love, because such a deed can never be undone. Richard may be a delusion of my brain. But how dull is reality! What a curse is a heart! With all to make me happy I pine and hanker for him, my other half, to fill this void, for I feel as if I were not complete. Is it wrong to want some one to love more than one's father and mother—on whom to lavish one's best feelings? What will my life be alone? I cannot marry any of the insignificant beings round me. Where are all those men who inspired the *grandes passions* of bygone days? Is the race extinct? Is Richard the last of them? Even so, is he for me? They point out the matches I might make if I took the trouble, but the trouble I will not take. I have no vocation to be a nun. I do not consider myself good enough to offer to God. God created me with a warm heart, a vivid imagination, and strong passions; God has given me food for hunger, drink for thirst, but no companion for my loneliness of heart. If I could only be sure of dying at forty, and until then preserve youth, health, spirits, and good looks, I should be more cheerful to remain as I am. I cannot separate myself from all thought of Richard. Neither do I expect God to work a miracle to make me happy. To me there are three kinds of marriage: first, worldly ambition; that is, marriage for fortune, title, estates, society; secondly, love; that is, the usual pig and cottage; thirdly, life, which is my ideal of being a companion and wife, a life of travel, adventure, and danger, seeing and learning, with love to glorify it; that is what I seek. *L'amour n'y manquerait pas!* . . .

One always pictures the "proper man" to be a rich, fat, mild lordling, living on his estate, whence, as his lady, one might rise to be a leader of Almack's. But I am much mistaken if I do not deserve a better fate. I could not live like a vegetable in the country. I cannot picture myself in a white apron, with a bunch of keys, scolding my maids, counting eggs and butter, with a good and portly husband (I detest fat men!) with a broad-brimmed hat and a large stomach. And I should not like to marry a country squire, nor a doctor, nor a lawyer (I hear the parchments crackle now), nor a parson, nor a clerk in a London office. God help me! A dry crust, privations, pain, danger for him I love would be better. Let me go with the husband of my choice to battle, nurse him in his tent, follow him under the fire of ten thousand muskets. I would be his companion through hardship and trouble, nurse him if wounded, work for him in his tent, prepare his meals when faint, his bed when weary, and be his guardian angel of comfort—a felicity too exquisite for words! There is something in some women that seems born for the knapsack. How many great thoughts are buried under ordinary circumstances, and splendid positions exist that are barren of them—thoughts that are stifled from a feeling that they are too bold to be indulged in! I thank God for the blessed gift of imagination, though it may be a source of pain. It counteracts the monotony of life. One cannot easily quit a cherished illusion, though it disgusts one with ordinary life. Who has ever been so happy in reality as in imagination? And how unblessed are they who have no imagination, unless they obtain their wishes in reality! I do not obtain, so I seek them in illusion. Sometimes I think I am not half grateful enough to my parents, I do not half enough for them, considering what they are to me. Although we are not wealthy, what do I lack, what kindness do I not receive? Yet I seem in a hurry to leave them. There is nothing I would not do to add to their comfort, and it would grieve me to the heart to forsake them; and yet if I knew for certain that I should never have my wish, I should repine sadly. I love a good daughter, and a good daughter makes a good wife. How can I reconcile these things in my mind? I am miserable, afraid to hope, and yet I dare not despair when I look at the state of my heart. But one side is so heavy as nearly to sink the other, and thus my *beaux jours* will pass away, and my Ideal Lover will not then think me worth his while. Shall I never be at rest with him to love and understand me, to tell me every thought and feeling, in far different scenes from these—under canvas before Rangoon— anywhere in Nature?

I would have every woman marry; not merely liking a man well enough to accept him for a husband, as some of our mothers teach us, and so cause many unhappy marriages, but loving him so holily that, wedded or not wedded, she feels she is his wife at heart. But perfect love, like perfect beauty, is rare. I would have her so loyal that, though she sees all his little faults herself, she takes care no one else sees them; yet she would as soon think of loving him less for them as ceasing to look up to heaven because there were a few clouds in the sky. I would have her so true, so fond, that she needs neither to burthen him with her love, nor vex him with her constancy, since both are self-existent, and entirely independent of anything he gives or takes away. Thus she will not marry him for liking, esteem, gratitude for his love, but from the fulness of her own love. If Richard and I never marry, God will cause us to meet in the next world; we cannot be parted; we belong to one another.

Despite all I have seen of false, foolish, weak attachments, unholy marriages, the after-life of which is rendered unholier still by struggling against the inevitable, still I believe in the one true love that binds a woman's heart faithful to one man in this life, and, God grant it, in the next. All this I am and could be for one man. But how worthless should I be for any other man but Richard Burton! I should love Richard's wild, roving, vagabond life; and as I am young, strong, and hardy, with good nerves, and no fine notions, I should be just the girl for him; I could never love anyone who was not daring and spirited. I always feel inclined to treat the generality of men just like my own sex. I am sure I am not born for a jog-trot life; I am too restless and romantic. I believe my sister and I have now as much excitement and change as most girls, and yet I find everything slow. I long to rush round the world in an express; I feel as if I shall go mad if I remain at home. Now with a soldier of fortune, and a soldier at heart, one would go everywhere, and lead a life worth living. What others dare I can dare. And why should I not? I feel that we women simply are born, marry, and die. Who misses us? Why should we not have some useful, active life? Why, with spirits, brains, and energies, are women to exist upon worsted work and household accounts? It makes me sick, and I will not do it.

From her diary for 1852.

Harriet Martineau

AND now my own special trial was at hand. It is not necessary to go into detail about it. The news which got abroad that we had grown comparatively poor, and the evident certainty that we were never likely to be rich, so wrought upon the mind of one friend as to break down the mischief which I have referred to as caused by ill-offices. My friend had believed me rich, was generous about making me a poor man's wife, and had been discouraged in more ways than one. He now came to me and we were virtually engaged. I was at first very anxious and unhappy. My veneration for his morale was such that I felt I dared not undertake the charge of his happiness; and yet I dared not refuse, because I saw it would be his death-blow. I was ill—I was deaf— I was in an entangled state of mind between conflicting duties and some lower considerations; and many a time did I wish, in my fear that I should fail, that I had never seen him. I am far from wishing that now; now that the beauty of his goodness remains to me, clear of all painful regrets. But there was a fearful period to pass through. Just when I was growing happy, surmounting my fears and doubts, and enjoying his attachment, the consequences of his long struggle and suspense overtook him. He became suddenly insane; and after months of illness of body and mind, he died. The calamity was aggravated to me by the unaccountable insults I received from his family, whom I had never seen. Years afterwards, when his sister and I met, the mystery was explained. His family had been given to understand, by cautious insinuations, that I was actually engaged to another, while receiving my friend's addresses! There has never been any doubt in my mind that, considering what I was in those days, it was happiest for us both that our union was prevented by any means.

I am, in truth, very thankful for not having married at all. I have never since been tempted, nor have suffered anything at all in relation to that matter which is held to be all-important for a woman—love and marriage. Nothing, I mean, beyond occasional annoyance, presently disposed of. Every literary woman, no doubt, has plenty of importunity of that sort to deal with; but freedom of mind and coolness of manner dispose of it very easily: and since the time I have been speaking of, my mind has been wholly free from all idea of love-affairs. My subsequent literary life in London was clear from all difficulty and embarrassment; no doubt because I was evidently too busy, and

too full of interests of other kinds, to feel any awkwardness—
to say nothing of my being then thirty years of age; an age at
which, if ever, a woman is certainly qualified to take care of herself. I can easily conceive how I might have been tempted—
how some deep springs in my nature might have been touched,
then or earlier; but, as a matter of fact, they never were; and I
consider the immunity a great blessing, under the liabilities of a
moral condition such as mine was in the olden time. If I had had
a husband dependent on me for his happiness, the responsibility
would have made me wretched. If my husband had *not* depended
on me for his happiness, I should have been jealous. So also with
children. The care would have so overpowered the joy—the love
would have so exceeded the ordinary chances of life—the fear
on my part would so have impaired the freedom on theirs, that
I rejoice not to have been involved in a relation for which I was,
or believed myself to be, unfit. The veneration in which I hold
domestic life has always shown me that that life was not for those
whose self-respect had been early broken down, or had never
grown. Happily, the majority are free from this disability.
Those who suffer under it had better be as I—as my observation
of married as well as single life assures me. When I see what
conjugal love is, in the extremely rare cases in which it is seen
in its perfection, I feel that there is a power of attachment in me
that has never been touched. When I am among little children,
it frightens me to think what my idolatry of my own children
would have been. But, through it all, I have ever been thankful
to be alone. My strong will, combined with anxiety of conscience,
makes me fit only to live alone; and my taste and liking are for
living alone. The older I have grown, the more serious and
irremediable have seemed to me the evils and disadvantages of
married life, as it exists among us at this time; and I am provided
with what it is the bane of single life in ordinary cases to want—
a substantial, laborious and serious occupation. My business in
life has been to think and learn, and to speak out with absolute
freedom what I have thought and learned. The freedom is
itself a positive and never-failing enjoyment to me, after the

bondage of my early life. My work and I have been fitted to each other, as is proved by the success of my work and my own happiness in it. The simplicity and independence of this vocation first suited my infirm and ill-developed nature, and then sufficed for my needs, together with family ties and domestic duties, such as I have been blessed with, and as every woman's heart requires. Thus, I am not only entirely satisfied with my lot, but think it the very best for me—under my constitution and circumstances: and I long ago came to the conclusion that, without meddling in the case of the wives and mothers, I am probably the happiest single woman in England. Who could have believed, in that awful year 1826, that such would be my conclusion a quarter of a century afterwards!

An Autobiography, 1855.

Maria Nugent

A NOTE from my dear N. to say that he will certainly be at home by 7 or 8 this evening. Order the servants a fête in consequence and, with the assistance of the Misses Murphy, make all my preparations in the best manner. Dined with the gentlemen of the family before 3, and immediately after take our stations in the Piazza, to see the blackies enjoy themselves.

A long table was spread on the green, with all their most favourite dishes, of barbecued hog, jerked hog, pepperpot, yams, plantains &c. There were tubs of punch, and each of them had three glasses of Madeira, to drink three toasts—"Massa Gubernor, and Missis, and little Massa"—all of which were drunk with three times three, by the men, women and children, and their sweethearts. The little children were all allowed a little sip, out of the grown up people's glasses.

As soon as the ceremony was over, I began the ball with an

old Negro man. The gentlemen each selected a partner, according to rank, by age or service, and we all danced. However, I was not aware how much I shocked the Misses Murphy by doing this; for I did exactly the same as I would have done at a servants' hall birthday in England. They told me, afterwards, that they were nearly fainting, and could hardly forbear shedding a flood of tears at such an unusual and extraordinary sight; for in this country, and among slaves, it was necessary to keep up so much more distant respect! They may be right. I meant nothing wrong, and all the poor creatures seemed so delighted, and so much pleased, that I could scarcely repent it. I was, nevertheless very sorry to have hurt their feelings, and particularly too as they seemed to think the example dangerous; as making the blacks of too much consequence, or putting them at all on a footing with the whites, they said, might make a serious change in their conduct, and even produce a rebellion in the Island.

But to proceed with my fête. I had people on the look-out for the arrival of my dear N., and about 8 o'clock his approach was announced. I then marched at the head of the whole party, with little George in my arms, to meet him; the music playing "God Save the King." As he got out of his carriage to join us, we saluted him, with three cheers. Dear Georgy was at first a little frightened with the noise and bustle, but he soon began to laugh, and appeared to enjoy all that was going forwards, as if he understood the whole thing. We had a little supper in the Piazza. The blackies resumed their dancing, and kept up their gaiety the greatest part of the night.

From her *Journal*, April 26th, 1803.

Dorothy Osborne

I KNOW not whether my letter were kind or not, but I'll swear yours was not, and am sure mine was meant to be so. It is not kind in you to desire an increase of my friendship; that is to doubt it is not as great already as it can be, than which you can do me no greater injury. 'Tis my misfortune that it lies not in my power to give you better testimonies of it than words, otherwise I should soon convince you that 'tis the best quality I have, and that where I own a friendship, I mean so perfect a one as time can neither lessen nor increase.

If I said nothing of my coming to town, 'twas because I had nothing to say that I thought you would like to hear. The truth is, twenty little cross accidents had made it so uncertain, that I was more out of humour with them than you could be with the bells; though I had no reason to expect otherwise, for I do not know that ever I desired anything, earnestly, in my life but 'twas. denied me, and I am many times afraid to wish a thing, merely lest my Fortune should take that occasion to use me ill. She cannot see, and therefore I may venture to write that I intend to be at London, if it be possible, on Friday or Saturday come sennight. Be sure you do not read it aloud, lest she hear it and prevent me, or drive you away, before I come.

It is so like my luck, too, that you should be going I know not whither again that, trust me, I have looked for it ever since I heard you were come home. You will laugh, sure, when I shall tell you that, hearing my Lord Lisle was to go Ambassador into Sweden, I remembered your father's acquaintance in that family, with an apprehension that he might be in the humour of sending you with him. But, for God's sake, whither is it that you go? I would not willingly be at such a loss again, as I was after your Yorkshire journey. If it prove a long one, I shall not forget you, but in earnest I shall be so possessed with a strong splenetic fancy that I shall never see you more in this world, as all the waters in England will not cure. Well, this is a sad story, we'll have no more of it.

A letter to Sir William Temple, written from
Chicksands in January 1653.

Lady Mary Wortley Montagu

THOUGH your letter is far from what I expected, having once promised to answer it with the sincere account of my inmost thoughts, I am resolved you shall not find me worse than my word, which is (whatever you may think) inviolable.

'Tis no affectation to say that I despise the pleasure of pleasing people whom I despise; all the fine equipages that shine in the ring never gave me another thought than either pity or contempt for their owners, that could place happiness in attracting the eyes of strangers. Nothing touches me with satisfaction but what touches my heart, and I should find more pleasure in the secret joy I should feel at a kind expression from a friend I esteemed than at the admiration of a whole playhouse, or the envy of those of my own sex, who could not attain to the same number of jewels, fine clothes etc., supposing I was at the very summit of this sort of happiness.

You may be this friend if you please: did you really esteem me, had you any tender regard for me, I could, I think, pass my life in any station happier with you than in all the grandeur of the world with any other. You have some humours that would be disagreeable to any woman that married with an intention of finding her happiness abroad. That is not my resolution. If I marry, I propose to myself a retirement; there is few of my acquaintance

I should ever wish to see again; and the pleasing one, and only one, is the way in which I design to please myself. Happiness is the natural design of all the world; and everything we see done is meant to attain it. My imagination places it in friendship. By friendship, I mean an entire communication of thoughts, wishes, interests and pleasures, being undivided; a mutual esteem, which naturally carries with it a pleasing sweetness of conversation, and terminates in the desire of making one another happy, without being forced to run into visits, noise and hurry, which serve rather to trouble than compose the thoughts of any reasonable creature. There are few capable of a friendship such as I have described, and 'tis necessary for the generality of the world to be taken up with trifles. Carry a fine lady or gentleman out of town, and they know no more what to say. To take from them plays, operas and fashions is taking away all their topics of discourse; and they know not how to form their thoughts on any other subjects. They know very well what it is to be admired, but are perpetually ignorant of what it is to be loved. I take you to have sense enough not to think this science romantic: I rather choose the word friendship than love, because in the general sense that word is spoke, it signifies a passion rather founded on fancy than reason: and when I say friendship, I mean a mixture of friendship and esteem, which a long acquaintance increases, not decays; how far I deserve such a friendship I can be no judge of myself: I may want the good sense that is necessary to be agreeable to a man of merit, but I know I want the vanity to believe I have; and can promise you shall never like me less, upon knowing me better; and that I shall never forget that you have a better understanding than myself.

And now let me entreat you to think (if possible) tolerably of my modesty after so bold a declaration. I am resolved to throw off reserve, and use me ill if you please. I am sensible to own an inclination for a man is putting oneself wholly in his power; but sure you have generosity enough not to abuse it. After all I have said, I pretend no tie but on your heart: if you do not love me, I shall not be happy with you; if you do, I need add no further.

I am not mercenary, and would not receive an obligation that comes not from one who loves me. I do not desire my letter back again; you have honour and I dare trust you. I am going to the same place I went last spring. I shall think of you there: it depends upon you in what manner.

A letter, written while she was still Lady Mary Pierrepont,
to Edward Wortley Montagu, in March 1711.

Anne Fanshawe

My husband had provided very good lodgings for us, and as soon as he could come home from the Council, where he was at my arrival, he with all expressions of joy received me in his arms, and gave me a hundred pieces of gold, saying "I know thou that keeps my heart so well, will keep my fortune, which from this time I will ever put into thy hands, as God shall bless me with increase." And now I thought myself a perfect queen, and my husband so glorious a crown, that I more valued myself to be called by his name than born a princess, for I knew him very wise and very good, and his soul doted on me; upon which confidence I will tell you what happened.

My Lady Rivers, a brave woman, and one that had suffered many thousand pounds loss for the King, and whom I had a great reverence for, and she a kindness for me as a kinswoman—in discourse she tacitly commended the knowledge of state affairs, and that some women were very happy in a good understanding thereof, as my Lady Aubigny, Lady Isabel Thynne, and divers others, and yet none was at first more capable than I; that in the night she knew that there came a post from Paris from the Queen, and that she would be extremely glad to hear what the Queen commanded the King in order to his affairs; saying, if I would ask my husband privately, he would tell me what he found in the packet, and I might tell her. I that was young and innocent, and to that day had never in my mouth what news, began to think there was more in inquiring into public affairs than I thought of, and that it being a fashionable thing would make me more beloved of my husband, if that had been possible, than I was.

When my husband returned home from Council, after welcoming him, as his custom ever was he went with his handful of papers into his study for an hour or more; I followed him; he turned hastily, and said, "What wouldst thou have, my life?" I told him, I had heard the Prince had received a packet from the Queen, and I guessed it was that in his hand, and I desired to know what was in it; he smilingly replied, "My love, I will immediately come to thee, pray thee go, for I am very busy." When he came out of his closet, I revived my suit; he kissed me and talked of other things. At supper I would eat nothing; he as usual sat by me, and drank often to me, which was his custom, and was full of discourse to company that was at table. Going to bed, I asked again, and said I could not believe he loved me if he refused to tell me all he knew; but he answered me nothing, but stopped my mouth with kisses. So we went to bed, I cried, and he went to sleep. Next morning early, as his custom was, he called to rise, but began to discourse with me first, to which I made no reply; he rose, came to the other side of the bed and kissed me, and drew the curtains softly and went to Court. When he came home to dinner, he presently came to me as usual, and when I had him by the hand, I said, "Thou dost not care to see me troubled"; to which he, taking me in his arms, answered, "My dearest soul, nothing upon earth can afflict me like that, and when you asked me of my business, it was wholly out of my power to satisfy thee, for my life and fortune shall be thine, and every thought of my heart in which the trust I am in may not be revealed; but my honour is my own, which I cannot preserve if I communicate the Prince's affairs; and pray thee with this answer rest satisfied." So great was his reason and goodness, that upon consideration it made my folly appear to me so vile, that from that day until the day of his death I never thought fit to ask him any business but what he communicated freely to me in order to his estate or family.

Memoirs of Lady Fanshawe.

Margaret Cavendish, Duchess of Newcastle

My Lord also recreates himself with his pen, writing what his wit dictates to him, but I pass my time rather with scribbling than writing, with words than wit, not that I speak much, because I am addicted to contemplation, unless I am with my Lord, yet then I rather attentively listen to what he says, than impertinently speak, yet when I am writing, and sad feigned stories, or serious humours, or melancholy passions, I am forced many times to express them with the tongue before I can write them with the pen, by reason those thoughts that are sad, serious and melancholy are apt to contract and to draw too much back, which oppression doth as it were overpower or smother the conception in the brain, but when some of those thoughts are set out in words, they give the rest more liberty to place themselves in a more methodical order, marching more regularly with my pen, on the ground of white paper, but my letters seem rather as a ragged rout than a well armed body, for the brain being quicker in creating than the hand in writing, or the memory in retaining, many fancies are lost, by reason they ofttimes outrun the pen; where I, to keep speed in the race, write so fast as I stay not so long as to write my letters plain, insomuch as some have taken my handwriting for some strange character, and being accustomed so to do, I cannot now write very plain, when I strive to write my best; indeed, my ordinary handwriting is so bad as few can read it, so as to write it fair for

the press, but howsoever, that little wit I have, it delights me to
scribble it out, and disperse it about, for I being addicted from
my childhood to contemplation rather than conversation, to
solitariness rather than society, to melancholy rather than mirth,
to write with the pen than to work with the needle, passing my
time with harmless fancies, their company being pleasing, their
conversation innocent, in which I take such pleasure as I neglect
my health, for it is as great a grief to leave their society, as a joy
to be in their company, my only trouble is, lest my brain should
grow barren, or that the root of my fancies should become insipid,
withering into a dull stupidity for want of maturing subjects to
write on; for I being of a lazy nature, and not of an active disposition, as some are that love to journey from town to town,
from place to place, from house to house, delighting in variety of
company, making still one where the greatest number is;
likewise in playing at cards, or in any other games, in which I
neither have practised, nor have I any skill therein; as for dancing,
although it be a graceful art, and becometh unmarried persons
well, yet for those that are married, it is too light an action, dis-
agreeing with the gravity thereof; and for revelling I am of too
dull a nature to make one in a merry society; as for feasting, it
would neither agree with my humour or constitution, for my
diet is for the most part sparing, as a little boiled chicken, or the
like, my drink most commonly water, for though I have an
indifferent good appetite, yet I do often fast, out of an opinion
that if I should eat much, and exercise little, which I do, only
walking a slow pace in my chamber, whilst my thoughts run
apace in my brain, so that the motions of my mind hinders the
active exercises of my body; for should I dance, or run, or walk
apace, I should dance my thoughts out of measure, run my
fancies out of breath, and tread out the feet of my numbers;
but because I would not bury myself quite from the sight of the
world, I go sometimes abroad, seldom to visit, but only in my
coach about the town, or about some of the streets . . . besides,
I do find that several objects do bring new materials for my
thoughts and fancies to build upon, yet I must say this on behalf

of my thoughts, that I never found them idle; for if the senses bring no work in, they will work of themselves, like silkworms that spin out of their own bowels; neither can I say I think the time tedious, when I am alone, so I be near my Lord, and know he is well.

A True Relation of the Birth, Breeding and Life of Margaret Cavendish, Duchess of Newcastle, written by herself.

Pastime and Good Company

———— ✺ ————

WILLIAM HICKEY

CHARLES LAMB

GEORGE MOORE

JOHN PAWSON

GEORGE-ANN BELLAMY

FANNY BURNEY

FANNY KEMBLE

COLLEY CIBBER

ROBERT BURNS

ADAM MARTINDALE

JOHN DUNTON

EDWARD LEAR

LORD HERBERT OF CHERBURY

GEORGE OSBALDESTON

MATTHEW PRIOR

W. H. DAVIES

JAMES BOSWELL

SAMUEL PEPYS

William Hickey

A BUSINESS was transacting in our office, whereon my father was extremely desirous of consulting Mr Thurlow. The matter pressed in point of time, not an hour was to be lost, and as two of the clerks who were sent in search of him had failed in their object, my father bid me try what I could do, and if I succeeded he would give me a guinea. Out I set, and as I had at the commencement of my clerkship made friends with most of the head waiters in the taverns and coffee houses in Chancery Lane, Fleet Street, and that part of the town, I felt confident I should obtain the promised reward, and did so, though after more difficulty than I expected.

After going the usual round in vain, I called upon the barmaid at Nando's, with whom I was a favourite, and entreated her to tell me where Mr Thurlow was. At first she protested she knew not, but by a little coaxing I got the secret, and proceeded to the Rolls Tavern, where I had already been, but there happening to be two new waiters who were of course unacquainted with me, they were faithful to their orders, and denied his being there. Upon my second visit I went into the bar, where addressing the landlord, I told him I had ascertained Mr Thurlow was in the house, and see him I must. The host was inflexible, and would not *peach*, but in a few minutes after I entered, he called out, "Charles, carry up half a dozen of red sealed port to No. 3."

It instantly struck me that must be the apartment my man was in, and as the waiter passed with the basket of wine, I pushed by him, ran up to No. 3, boldly opened the door, and there sat Mr Thurlow and four other gentlemen at a table with bottles and glasses before them. Upon seeing me he exclaimed, "Well, you young scoundrel, damn your blood, what do you want?

How the devil did you find me out? Take away your papers, for I'll be damned if I look at one of them. Come, come, you scoundrel, I know what you came for; you take after your father and are a damned drunken hog, so here, drink of this," filling a tumbler of wine which I had not the smallest objection to, and drank the health of the company. "But how did you find me out?" asked Mr Thurlow.

"Why, sir," answered I, "I heard the master of the house order six bottles of port for No. 3, and I was certain there you must be, so I ran up and entered without ceremony."

This made a great laugh, putting Mr Thurlow into high good humour, who swore I was a damned clever fellow, and should do, and turning to his companions he said—"This is a wicked dog, who does with me as he pleases, a son of Joe Hickey."

I was thereupon particularly noticed by them all, and pulling out my papers Mr Thurlow looked them over and immediately wrote a note to my father upon the subject, which I carried home, thereby gaining not only the promised guinea, but credit for the manner in which I had effected the business.

Memoirs.

Charles Lamb

I OUGHT to have replied to your very kind invitation into Cumberland. With you and your sister I could gang anywhere. But I am afraid whether I shall ever be able to afford so desperate a journey. Separate from the pleasure of your company, I don't much care if I never see a mountain in my life. I have passed all my days in London, until I have formed as many and intense local attachments, as any of you mountaineers can have done with dead nature. The lighted shops of the Strand and Fleet Street, the innumerable trades, tradesmen and customers, coaches, waggons, playhouses, all the bustle and wickedness round about Covent Garden, the very women of the town, the watchmen, drunken scenes, rattles—life awake, if you awake, at all hours of the night, the impossibility of being dull in Fleet Street, the crowds, the very dirt and mud, the sun shining upon houses and pavements, the print shops, the old book stalls, parsons cheapening books, coffee houses, steams of soups from kitchens, the pantomimes, London itself a pantomime and a masquerade— all these things work themselves into my mind and feed me, without a power of satiating me. The wonder of these sights impels me into night-walks about her crowded streets, and I often shed tears in the motley Strand from fulness of joy at so much Life. All these emotions must be strange to you. So are your rural emotions to me. But consider what must I have been doing all my life, not to have lent great portions of my heart with usury to such scenes?

My attachments are all local, purely local. I have no passion (or have had none since I was in love, and then it was the spurious engendering of poetry and books) to groves and valleys. The rooms where I was born, the furniture which has been before my eyes all my life, a book case which has followed me about (like a faithful dog, only exceeding him in knowledge) wherever I have moved—old chairs, old tables, streets, squares, where I have sunned myself, my old school—these are my mistresses. Have I not enough, without your mountains? I do not envy you. I should pity you, did I not know that the Mind will make friends of any thing. Your sun and moon and skies and hills and lakes affect me no more, or scarcely come to me in more venerable characters, than as a gilded room with tapestry and tapers, where I might live with handsome visible objects. I consider the clouds above me but as a roof, beautifully painted but unable to satisfy the mind, and at last, like the pictures of the apartment of a connoisseur, unable to afford him any longer a pleasure. So fading upon me, from disuse, have been the Beauties of Nature, as they have been confinedly called; so ever fresh and green and warm are all the inventions of men and assemblies of men in this great city.

A letter to William Wordsworth, January 30th, 1801.

George Moore

BALZAC was the great moral influence of my life, and my reading culminated in the *Comédie Humaine*. I no doubt fluttered through some scores of other books, of prose and verse, sipping a little honey, but he alone left any important or lasting impression on my mind. The rest was like walnuts and wine, an agreeable after-taste.

But notwithstanding all this reading, I can lay no claim to scholarship of any kind; for save life I could never learn anything correctly. I am a student only of ballrooms, bar-rooms, streets, and alcoves. I have read very little; but all I read I can turn to account, and all I read I remember. To read freely, extensively, has always been my ambition, and my utter inability to study has always been to me a subject of grave inquietude—study as contrasted with a general and haphazard gathering of ideas taken in flight. But in me the impulse is so original to frequent the haunts of men that it is irresistible, conversation is the breath of my nostrils, I watch the movement of life, and my ideas spring from it uncalled for, as buds from branches. Contact with the world is in me the generating force; without this what invention I have is thin and sterile, and it grows thinner rapidly, until it dies away utterly. . . .

Confessions of a Young Man, 1888.

John Pawson

ON our way (to Manchester) we were detained at Newark-upon-Trent on the Lord's day. Being obliged to take up our abode at an inn, we were rather at a loss, as we knew of no religious people in that town. We walked into the stable, and I asked the ostler if there were any Dissenters in that town? He said, he did not know, but there wanted something to reform the people, for they were very wicked. I replied, "You say you do not know whether there are any Dissenters; then you have not lived here long? Pray where do you come from?" He replied, "From Malton, in Yorkshire." I asked, "Pray, do you know Mr Wilson, of Malton?" "Yes," said the man, "and I know you, too; I have heard you preach there."

We walked into the churchyard in search of serious people. I though I saw a person who looked more solid than ordinary, and walked towards him. The man looked rather earnestly upon me, and said, "Pray, sir, are you upon a journey?" I answered, "Yes." "So am I," said he; "but pray, sir, are you not a preacher? I answered, "I am." "A Methodist preacher?" said he. I replied, "Yes." "Pray what is your name?" I answered, "My name is Pawson." "John Pawson," he replied, "I have heard you preach at Northallerton. I was looking about for some serious person, as I am quite a stranger in this place."

How condescendingly kind is our gracious God! We were looking about for a religious person, the honest stranger was doing the same, and the Lord granted out joint desire and brought us together. After the service of the church, we returned to our inn. I soon observed that the waiter was remarkably attentive to all we said; and as our conversation was wholly on religion, I perceived that he took particular note of it. In a while he ventured to speak, and said, "Gentlemen, we have a very good church in the town, and a tolerably good minister too, if you choose to go." I replied, "Yes, we have been at church this forenoon; we think it right to attend public worship at all opportunities; have you any religious people in this town?" "Very few indeed, sir," said he, "and the few there are, they call them Methodists. I know of only one woman, and myself, and they call us Methodists, although I never saw one in my life that I know of; but I have been led to think they are very good people, because they are so much hated and despised by the wicked." I replied, "I am inclined to think that you have formed a right judgment of them; I believe the Methodists in general fear the Lord, and endeavour to honour and obey him." "I have heard much," added he, "of Messrs. Whitefield and Wesley; but I am surprised that they should preach out of the church. And likewise they preach without a book; I wonder how the people can understand them." I replied, "You know our Lord preached upon a mountain, and St Paul in the house of one Justus, and in the school of one Tyrannus. And as to their preaching extemporary, I suppose the people may understand them the better, as they adapt their discourses to the capacities as well as the states of their hearers. I am a Methodist preacher, and so is my fellow-traveller. I preached in the streets at Norwich only last Lord's day." "Are you, sir?" said the man, "I have lived seven years at this house, and I never remember to have seen a religious person call here before, except the Bishop of Durham: he appeared to be a serious man." It is impossible to describe the delight this honest young man appeared to take in our company. He told us of his experience, and how he spent his time. It was evident that the Lord had graciously visited his soul, though he had never heard a Gospel sermon in his life, and had only the Bible, the Common Prayer Book, and Milton's *Paradise Lost* to read. He spent all the time he could possibly spare with us, willingly joined us in prayer, and would needs treat us with a bottle of wine, but this we refused. We thought it a little remarkable that, strangers as we were in the place, the

Lord should, in so particular a manner, direct us to, it seems, the only religious persons in the town.

The Life of Mr John Pawson, included in *The Lives of Early Methodist Preachers, chiefly written by themselves*, 1837.

George Anne Bellamy

HAVING crossed the ferry, Mr Crump and myself arrived at Bangor some time before the rest of the company; where the mistress of the inn accommodated me with even a shift and stockings. In all the countries through which I ever travelled, I never met with such civil people as at Welsh inns. There is a cordiality in their manners, which must give a susceptible mind the greatest pleasure. Uncontaminated with the self-interested attention of those who belong to more frequented inns, where every civility must be purchased, they cheerfully supply you with every accommodation in their power and are happy in obliging.

As soon as I was apparelled in my linsey-wolsey, which I assure you I found very comfortable, I joined my fellow-traveller, Mr Crump, to return him thanks for the care and civility he had shewn me. He had prepared a good fire in the parlour against my return, which was evidently done with the opportunity of getting me alone. His anxiety to do this must have been apparent to everyone but myself. Had I observed it, I should have thought him guilty of an unpardonable presumption. For a man of his years, and without one personal attraction, to presume to look to my *divinity-ship*, was a supposition I could form no idea of. I could not, however, help remarking that my companion, who had hitherto been very loquacious, was now altogether as silent. As I was much fatigued, and not very well able to keep up a conversation, I was not displeased at his taciturnity.

After prancing about the room for some time, he approached me, and with a deep-fetched sigh, which would have blown the boat we had lately entered over the river, without the assistance of the ferry-man, took hold of my hand. I perceived that he was much agitated, a circumstance which, though it might have been agreeable in a favoured lover, was very unbecoming in a person with whom I had been so newly acquainted. At length he summoned up resolution enough thus to address me: "My dear Miss Bellamy," said he, "answer me one question: were you ever in love?" My surprise at having such an interrogation put to me, and in so abrupt a manner, prevented me from making an immediate reply; but recollecting myself, I answered, "Oh! yes, violently." "Are you really attached?" said he. "*For ever*," returned I. "It would perhaps be deemed impertinent," continued the gentleman, "were I to presume to ask with whom?" I told him, I did not think it could be of any consequence to him; but if it was, I would gratify his curiosity, by informing him that it was—*with myself*. That I was a female Narcissus, and should always continue so. He had just the time to exclaim, "Then I am satisfied," when our company entered.

*From: An Apology for the Life of George Anne Bellamy, late of
Covent Garden Theatre, written by herself, 1785.*

Fanny Burney

I OFTEN think, when I am counting my laurels, what a pity it would have been had I popped off in my last illness, without knowing what a person of consequence I was!—and I sometimes think that, were I now to have a relapse, I could never go off with so much *éclat*!

. . . But Dr Johnson's approbation!—it almost crazed me with agreeable surprise—it gave me such a flight of spirits, that I danced a jig to Mr Crisp, without any preparation, music or explanation—to his no small amazement and diversion. I left him, however, to make his own comments upon my friskiness, without affording him the smallest assistance. . . .

A letter to her sister Susan, written in July 1778.

Fanny Kemble

MY mother, who had left the stage for upwards of twenty years, determined to return to it on the night of my first appearance, that I might have the comfort and support of her being with me in my trial. We drove to the theatre very early, indeed while the late autumn sunlight yet lingered in the sky; it shone into the carriage upon me, and as I screened my eyes from it, my mother said, "Heaven smiles on you, my child."

My poor mother went to her dressing-room to get herself ready, and did not return to me for fear of increasing my agitation by her own. My dear Aunt Dall and my maid and the theatre dresser performed my toilet for me, and at length I was placed in a chair with my satin train carefully laid over the back of it; and there I sat, ready for execution, with the palms of my hands pressed convulsively together, and the tears I in vain endeavoured to repress welling up into my cycs and brimming slowly over, down my rouged cheeks—upon which my aunt, with a smile full of pity, renewed the colour as often as these heavy drops made unsightly streaks in it. Once and again my father came to the door, and I heard his anxious "How is she?" to which my aunt answered, sending him away with words of comforting cheer.

At last, "Miss Kemble called for the stage, ma'am!" accompanied with a brisk tap at the door, started me upright on my feet, and I was led round to the side opposite to the one from which I saw my mother advance on the stage; and while the

139

uproar of her reception filled me with terror, dear old Mrs Davenport, my Nurse, and dear Mr Keely, her Peter, and half the *dramatis personae* of the play (but not my father, who had retreated, quite unable to endure the scene) stood round me as I lay, all but insensible, in my aunt's arms. "Courage, courage, dear child! Poor thing, poor thing!" reiterated Mrs Davenport. "Never mind 'em, Miss Kemble!" urged Keely, in that irresistibly comical, nervous, lachrymose voice of his, which I have never since heard without a thrill of anything but comical association; "Never mind 'em! Don't think of 'em, any more than if they were so many rows of cabbages!" "Nurse!" called my mother, and on waddled Mrs Davenport, and turning back, called in her turn, "Juliet!"

My aunt gave me an impetus forward, and I ran straight across the stage, stunned with the tremendous shout that greeted me, my eyes covered with mist, and the green baize flooring of the stage feeling as if it rose up against my feet; but I got hold of my mother, and stood like a terrified creature at bay, confronting the huge theatre full of gazing human beings. I do not think a word I uttered during this scene could have been audible; in the next, the ball-room, I began to forget myself; in the following one, I had done so, and, for aught I knew, I was Juliet; the passion I was uttering sending hot waves of blushes all over my neck and shoulders, while the poetry sounded like music to me as I spoke it, utterly transporting me into the imaginary existence of the play.

After this, I did not return into myself until all was over, and amid a thunderous storm of applause, congratulations, tears, embraces, and a general joyous explosion of unutterable relief at the fortunate termination of my attempt, we went home.

And so my life was determined, and I devoted myself to an avocation which I never liked or honoured, and about the very nature of which I have never been able to come to any decided opinion. It is in vain that the undoubted specific gifts of great actors and actresses suggest that all gifts are given for rightful exercise, and not for suppression; in vain that Shakespeare's plays urge their imperative claim to the most perfect illustration they can receive from histrionic interpretation; a *business* which is incessant excitement and factitious emotion seems to me unworthy of a man: a business which is public exhibition, unworthy of a woman.

Record of a Girlhood, 1878.

Colley Cibber

Now, sir, as I have been making my way for above forty years through a crowd of cares (all which by the favour of Providence I have honestly got rid of), is it a time of life for me to leave off these fooleries and to set up a new character? Can it be worth my while to waste my spirits, to bake my blood with serious contemplation, and perhaps impair my health, in the fruitless study of advancing myself into the better opinion of those very, very few wise men that are as old as I am? No, the part I have acted in real life shall be all of a piece . . . I will not go out of my character, by straining to be wiser than I can be, or by being more affectedly pensive than I need be; whatever I am, men of sense will know me to be, put on what disguise I will; I can no more put off my follies than my skin; I have often tried, but they stick too close to me; nor am I sure my friends are displeased with them; for besides that in this light I afford them frequent matter of mirth, they may possibly be less uneasy at their own foibles, when they have so old a precedent to keep them in countenance; nay, there are some frank enough to confess that they envy what they laugh at; and when I have seen others, whose rank and fortune have laid a sort of restraint upon their liberty of pleasing their company by pleasing themselves, I have said softly to myself, —"Well, there is some advantage in having neither rank nor fortune." . . .

141

Give me the joy I always took in the end of an old song—
My mind, my mind is a kingdom to me!

If I can please myself with my own follies, have not I a plentiful
provision for life? If the world thinks me a trifler, I do not
desire to break upon their wisdom; let them call me any fool but
an uncheerful one; I live as I write; while my way amuses me,
it is as well as I wish it; when another writes better, I can like
him too, though he should not like me. . . .

An Apology for the Life of Mr Colley Cibber, 1740.

Robert Burns

But, first an' foremost, I should tell,
Amaist as soon as I could spell,
I to the crambo-jingle fell;
    Tho' rude an' rough,
Yet crooning to a body's sel
    Does weel eneugh.

I am nae poet, in a sense,
But just a rhymer, like, by chance,
An' hae to learning nae pretence,
    Yet what the matter?
Whene'er my Muse does on me glance,
    I jingle at her.

Your critic-folk may cock their nose,
And say 'How can you e'er propose,
You wha ken hardly verse frae prose,
    To mak a sang?'
But, by your leaves, my learned foes,
    Ye're maybe wrang.

What's a' your jargon o' your schools,
Your Latin names for horns an' stools;
If honest Nature made you fools,
    What sairs your grammars?
Ye'd better ta'en up spades and shools,
    Or knappin'-hammers.

A set o' dull conceited hashes
Confuse their brains in college classes!
They gang in stirks, and come out asses,
    Plain truth to speak;
An' syne they think to climb Parnassus
    By dint o' Greek!

Gie me ae spark o' Nature's fire,
That's a' the learning I desire;
Then tho' I drudge thro' dub an' mire
    At pleugh or cart,
My Muse, though hamely in attire,
    May touch the heart.

O for a spunk o' Allan's glee,
Or Fergusson's, the bauld an' slee,
Or bright Lapraik's my friend to be,
    If I can hit it!
That would be lear eneugh for me,
    If I could get it.

Now, sir, if ye hae friends enow,
Tho' real friends, I b'lieve, are few,
Yet, if your catalogue be fou,
    I'se no insist,
But gif ye want ae friend that's true,
    I'm on your list.

I winna blaw about mysel,
As ill I like my fauts to tell;
But friends, an' folks that wish me well,
    They sometimes roose me;
Tho' I maun own, as mony still
    As far abuse me.

There's ae wee faut they whiles lay to me,
I like the lasses—Gude forgie me!
For many a plack they wheedle frae me,
    At dance or fair;
Maybe some ither thing they gie me
    They weel can spare.

But Mauchline race, or Mauchline fair,
I should be proud to meet you there;
We'se gie ae night's discharge to care,
    If we foregather,
An' hae a swap o' rhymin'-ware
    Wi' ane anither.

The four-gill chap, we'se gar him clatter,
An' kirsen him wi' reekin water;
Syne we'll sit down an' take our whitter,
    To cheer our heart;
An faith, we'se be acquainted better
    Before we part . . .

From *Epistle to John Lapraik, an old Scottish Bard.* Written
in April 1785.

Adam Martindale

WHEN this costly business was over, my back-friends took care I should not live without disturbance (though sometimes they played but at small game). The rabble of profane youths, and some doting fools that took their part, were encouraged to affront me, by setting up a May-pole in my way to the church, upon a little bank called Bow-hillock, where in times past the Sabbath had been woefully profaned (as tradition goes) by music and dancing; and where, in my time, there was a randez-vous of rake-hells, till I took an effectual way to stop them. I would not, for a time, seem to gratify their spiteful humour by taking notice of it; but in due season, when their youthful rage had somewhat cooled, and there was no colour to say what I spoke proceeded from passion, I took occasion to preach upon Prov. 1.22., *How long, ye simple ones, will ye love simplicity?* etc. and after I had laid before them many other things of greater weight, I calmly reproved their folly in erecting a May-pole in that way they had done; told them, many learned men were of opinion that a May-pole was a relic of the shameful worship of the Strumpet Flora in Rome; but however it was, it was a thing that never did, nor could do good; yea, had occasioned, and might occasion, much harm to people's souls; and I think I also told them of their sin in doing such a thing (though it were granted to be harmless in itself) on purpose to affront me, their spiritual father and pastor. This sermon somewhat nettled some of them; and to clear themselves that they were no friends to profaneness, they resolved, upon their own interest, to procure Mr Brooke, of Congleton (who had formerly preached at Rolleston and Leigh eight years, and was so well respected in the parish, and by me, that they knew I would not hinder him) to bestow his pains upon a Lord's day with us. Well! they prevailed and he came: but when he saw the May-pole in his way, and understood by whom and to what end it was set up, he did most smartly reprove their sin and folly, calling them by the most opprobrious names: as the scum, rabble, riff-raff (or such like) of the parish; insomuch that my words were smooth like oil in comparison of his, so full of salt and vinegar.

The Life of Adam Martindale, written by himself.

John Dunton

AND now, Reader, having in these sheets given ye the character of the chief booksellers in the three kingdoms, I hope you'll pardon me if in the last place I allow myself a character among the rest. 'Tis true, Cowley says, *The Voyage Life is longest made at home;* however, from that small acquaintance I have with myself, I may venture to say: As to my birth I count it no small honour that I descended from the Tribe of Levi ... so that I think myself more honoured in having a minister for my father, than if he had been a duke.

From this account of my birth, I proceed to a description of my person, which is So-So; however, two of the fair sex have been tempted to take it for better, for worse, and I don't hear they ever repented of their bargain, for I'm very uxurious by my natural temper and can (passionately) dote on a wife that has but one obliging quality.

Having given this account of my person, I shall next tell ye with what soul 'tis acted. This house of mine is filled with a rambling tenant, and being born to travel, I am ever pursuing my destiny; so that you may call me a Citizen of London and of the World; yet where e'er I come, I love to be guessed at, not

known, and to see the world unseen; and for that reason, I'm
now learning the art of living incognito. I must here (to my
mortification) reckon myself among the number of scribblers,
for my present income would not support me, did I not stoop so
low as to turn author; but, I find, 'tis what I was born to, for I
am a willing and everlasting drudge to the quill, and am now
writing A Farewell to Trade. My constant sickness and debts
have rather made me an author, than soldier, of fortune, and
therefore I'm very thankful to that kind muse that assists the
unfortunate: for could I not compose a few sheets for the press, I
might now starve, for 'tis not two years rent of my whole estate
will repair the damage I received by the late storm; and therefore as I now scratch my head for a living (and with the thread-
bare tribe, live in rhyme), 'tis a comfort I am wholly at the mercy
of that kind Samaritan, the Reverend Mr ***, who being a man of
true compassion and goodness will never stain his cloth etc,
for he knows in a few years I shall pay him all, and everybody
else, to a half farthing. . . .

I own I'm very rash in my actions, and scarce ever did anything (save taking two women, for better for worse) but I
repented of, one time or other. I have a great deal of mercury in
my natural temperament, for which I must have allowance; but
the best men are the most charitable, and no man (if he considers
himself) will blame that in me which I can't help; but baiting
this fault (though I say't myself) I'm as fit to make a friend as any
man; for when my friend falls to decay, I'm ready to rejoice (I
ask his pardon) that I have an opportunity to convince him I
loved in earnest, and though 'twere impossible he should ever
requite me, while I have anything, my friend shall have it all.
Nay, I have this peculiar to myself, that I love a friend the better
for being poor, miserable or despised. I confess, this looks a little
satirical to my summer-friends, but it is so great a truth, that
I can prove it by several persons now living in London. . . .

To sum up my character in a few words: I love travelling,
don't love fighting; love (my wife) Valeria, don't love money;
love my friend, don't fear or hate my enemy; love writing,

don't love starving; love fair dealing; had rather be called fool than knave; let people laugh when I win; can be secret if trusted (or woe be to Parson Grub); am owed more than I owe, and can pay more than that; make my word as good as my bond; won't do a foul thing; can live in a cell, till I pay my debts, and bid the world go whistle.

The Life and Errors of John Dunton, Late Citizen of London, Written by Himself in Solitude, With an Idea of a New Life; Wherein is Shewn How he'd Think, Speak and Act, Might he Live over his Days again: Intermix'd with the New Discoveries The Author has made In his Travels Abroad, and in his Private Conversations at Home. Together with the Lives and Characters of a Thousand Persons now living in London etc. Digested into Seven Stages with their Respective Ideas. 1705.

Edward Lear

How pleasant to know Mr Lear,
    Who has written such volumes of stuff!
Some think him ill-tempered and queer,
    But a few think him pleasant enough.

His mind is concrete and fastidious,
    His nose is remarkably big;
His visage is more or less hideous,
    His beard it resembles a wig.

He has ears, and two eyes, and ten fingers,
    Leastways if you reckon two thumbs;
Long ago he was one of the singers,
    But now he is one of the dumbs.

EDWARD LEAR

He sits in a beautiful parlour,
  With hundreds of books on the wall;
He drinks a great deal of Marsala,
  But never gets tipsy at all.

He has many friends, laymen and clerical;
  Old Foss is the name of his cat;
His body is perfectly spherical,
  He weareth a runcible hat.

When he walks in a waterproof white,
  The children run after him so!
Calling, out, "He's come out in his night-
  Gown, that crazy old Englishman, oh!"

He weeps by the side of the ocean,
  He weeps on the top of the hill;
He purchases pancakes and lotion,
  And chocolate shrimps from the mill.

He reads but he cannot speak Spanish,
  He cannot abide ginger-beer:
Ere the days of his pilgrimage vanish,
  How pleasant to know Mr Lear!
        Nonsense Songs, Stories and Botany, 1870.

Lord Herbert of Cherbury

I SHALL relate now some things concerning myself, which, though they may seem scarce credible, yet before God are true. I had been in France about a year and a half when my tailor, Andrew Henly of Basil, who now lives in Blackfriars, demanded of me half a yard of satin to make me a suit more than I was accustomed to give, of which I required a reason, saying I was not fatter than when I came to France. He answered, it was true, but you are taller; whereunto when I would give no credit, he brought his old measures, and made it appear that they did not reach to their just places. I told him I knew not how this happened, but howsoever he should have half a yard more, and when I came into England I would clear the doubt; for a little before my departure thence I remember William Earl of Pembroke and myself did measure heights together at the request of the Countess of Bedford, and he was then higher than I by about the breadth of my little finger. At my return therefore into England I measured again with the same earl, and to both our great wonders found myself taller than he by the breadth of a little finger; which growth of mine I could attribute to no other cause but to my quartan ague formerly mentioned, which, when it quitted me, left me in a more perfect health than I formerly enjoyed, and indeed disposed me to some follies which I afterwards repented, and do still repent of; but as my wife refused to come over, and my temptations were great, I hope that faults I committed are the more pardonable. Howsoever, I can say truly that whether in France or England, I was never in a bawdyhouse, nor used my pleasures intemperately, and much less did accompany them with that dissimulation and falsehood which is commonly found in men addicted to love women. To conclude this passage, which I unwillingly mention, I must protest again before God, that I never delighted in that or any other kind of sin, and that if I transgressed sometimes in this kind, it was to avoid a greater ill; for certainly if I had been provided with a lawful remedy, I should have fallen into no extravagancy. I could extenuate my fault, by telling circumstances which would have operated, I doubt, upon the chastest of mankind, but I forbear, those things are not to be spoken of; for though the philosophers have accounted this act to be *inter honestu factu*, where neither injury nor violence was offered, yet they ever reckoned it among the *turpia dictu*. I shall therefore only tell some other things alike strange of myself.

I weighed myself in balances often with men lower than my-self by the head, and in their bodies slenderer, and yet was found lighter than they, as Sir John Danvers, knight, and Richard Griffiths, now living, can witness, with both whom I have been weighed. I had also, and have still, a pulse on the crown of my head. It is well known to those that wait in my chamber, that the shirts, waistcoats and other garments I wear next my body are sweet, beyond what either easily can be believed, or hath been observed in any else; which sweetness also was found to be in my breath above others, before I used to take tobacco, which towards my latter time I was forced to take against certain rheums and catarrhs that trouble me, which yet did not taint my breath for any long time. I scarce ever felt cold in my life, though yet so subject to catarrhs, that I think no man ever was more obnoxious to it. All which I do in a familiar way mention to my posterity, though otherwise they might be thought scarce worth the writing.

An Autobiography.

George Osbaldeston

I WAS never able to understand the military point of view; having been Jack of all trades. I was once an officer myself. It was about fifty years ago when the local militia was first embodied in Yorkshire, and a gentleman by the name of Fother-gill, who owned considerable property and lived within ten miles of my residence, was appointed colonel. He had been in the army for many years, therefore was a very proper person for such an appointment. I was lieut-colonel under him; not on account of any military knowledge I possessed, but merely because owing to my large estates in that part of the kingdom, I had influence in the neighbourhood. Our major and captain were nearly as great novices as myself, and the colonel had a most responsible office. He was a testy old file, very fidgety, and not at all a favourite among his officers. The regiment was quartered at Scarborough, which has now become a very beautiful watering-place and a borough. There is a very high rock on the north side of the town, upon which are some barracks, generally occupied by regular troops, and in front is a grass space on which we were exercised. All the officers, barring old Colonel "Testy", were well pleased when our training and drilling were over, though we had got on tolerably well until the old crab was taken ill, so that I had to take command of the regiment.

I was not at all competent to discharge the duties of colonel, so I applied to the adjutant, who had been in the Regular Army; and he stood by me on parade and instructed me as to the commands I ought to give, and saw that they were executed. We managed to get on all right at drill; but I failed, I suppose, as a disciplinarian. It was in this way. The men had to rest for an hour or two between different parts of their drilling, and did not seem to know what to do with themselves; so to amuse them I got up races, jumping in sacks, and so on, which they enjoyed. This, it appeared, was not at all a proper thing to do; for when, after two days, the colonel got well and resumed command, he was exceedingly angry at my proceedings, and termed them a breach of military duty. I don't remember the expressions he used about me before all the men assembled on parade, but I know they were not complimentary.

Squire Osbaldeston: his Autobiography.

Matthew Prior

For my own Monument

As doctors give physic by way of prevention
  Matt alive and in health of his tomb-stone took care,
For delays are unsafe, and his pious intention
  May haply be never fulfilled by his heir.

Then take Matt's word for it, the sculptor is paid,
  That the figure is fine, pray believe your own eye,
Yet credit but lightly what more may be said,
  For we flatter our selves, and teach marble to lie.

Yet counting as far as to fifty his years,
  His virtues and vices were as other men's are,
High hopes he conceiv'd, and he smother'd great fears,
  In a life parti-colour'd, half pleasure, half care.

Nor to business a drudge, nor to faction a slave,
  He strove to make int'rest and freedom agree,
In public employments industrious and grave,
  And alone with his friends, Lord, how merry was he.

Now in equipage stately, now humbly on foot,
  Both fortunes he tried, but to neither would trust,
And whirl'd in the round, as the wheel turn'd about,
  He found riches had wings, and knew man was but dust.

This verse little polish'd, though mighty sincere,
  Sets neither his titles nor merit to view;
It says that his relics collected lie here,
  And no mortal yet knows too if this may be true.

Fierce robbers there are that infest the highway,
  So Matt may be kill'd, and his bones never found;
False witness at court, and fierce tempests at sea,
  So Matt may yet chance to be hang'd, or be drown'd.

If his bones lie in earth, roll in sea, fly in air,
  To Fate we must yield, and the thing is the same;
And if passing thou giv'st him a smile, or a tear,
  He cares not—yet prythee be kind to his fame.

Miscellaneous Works, 1740.

W. H. Davies

THE train whistled almost before we were ready, and pulled slowly out of the station. I allowed my companion the advantage of being the first to jump, owing to his maimed hand. The train was now going faster, and we were forced to keep pace with it. Making a leap, he caught the handle bar and sprang lightly on the step, after which my hand quickly took possession of the bar, and I ran with the train, prepared to follow his example. To my surprise, instead of at once taking his place on the platform, my companion stood thoughtlessly irresolute on the step, leaving me no room to make the attempt. But I still held to the bar, though the train was now going so fast that I found great difficulty in keeping step with it. I shouted to him to clear the step. This he proceeded to do, very deliberately, I thought. Taking a firmer grip on the bar, I jumped, but it was too late, for the train was now going at a rapid rate. My foot came short of the step and I fell and, still clinging to the handle bar, was dragged several yards before I relinquished my hold. And there I lay for several minutes, feeling a little shaken, whilst the train passed swiftly on into the darkness.

Even then I did not know what had happened, for I attempted to stand, and found that something had happened to prevent me from doing this. Sitting down in an upright position, I then began to examine myself, and now found that the right foot was severed from the ankle. This discovery did not shock me so much as the thoughts which quickly followed. For, as I could feel no pain, I did not know but what my body was in several parts, and I was not satisfied until I had examined every portion of it. Seeing a man crossing the track, I shouted to him for assistance. He looked in one direction and another, not seeing me in the darkness, and was going his way when I shouted again. This time he looked full my way, but instead of coming nearer, he made one bound in the air, nearly fell, scrambled to his feet, and was off like the shot of a gun. This man was sought after for several weeks, by people curious to know who he was, but was never found, and no man came forward to say, "I am he." Having failed to find this man, people at last began to think I was under a ghostly impression. Probably that was the other man's impression, for who ever saw Pity make the same speed as Fear?

Another man, after this, approached, who was a workman on the line, and at the sound of my voice he seemed to understand at once what had occurred. Coming forward quickly, he looked me over, went away, and in a minute or two returned with the assistance of several others to convey me to the station. A number of people were still there; so that when I was placed in the waiting room to bide the arrival of a doctor, I could see no other way of keeping a calm face before such a number of eyes than by taking out my pipe and smoking, an action which, I am told, caused much sensation in the local press.

I bore this accident with an outward fortitude that was far from the true state of my feelings. The doctor, seeing the even development of my body, asked me if I was an athlete. Although I could scarcely claim to be one, I had been able, without any training, and at any time, to jump over a height of five feet; had also been a swimmer and, when occasion offered, had donned the gloves. Thinking of my present helplessness caused me many a bitter moment, but I managed to impress all comers with a false indifference.

What a kind-hearted race of people are these Canadians! Here was I, an entire stranger among them, and yet every hour people were making enquiries, and interesting themselves on my behalf, bringing and sending books, grapes, bananas and other delicacies for a sick man. When a second operation was deemed necessary, the leg to be amputated at the knee, the whole town was concerned, and the doctor had to give strict injunctions not to admit such a number of kind-hearted visitors.

At this time I was so weak of body that it was thought hopeless to expect recovery from this second operation. This was soon made apparent to me, by the doctor's question, as to whether I had any message to send to my people, hinting that there was a slight possibility of dying under the chloroform. A minister of the gospel was also there, and his sympathetic face certainly made the dying seem probable. Now, I have heard a great deal of dying men having a foresight of things to be, but I confess that I was never more calm in all my life than at this moment when death seemed so certain. I did not for one instant believe or expect that these eyes would again open to the light, after I had been in this low vital condition, deadened and darkened for over two hours, while my body was being cut and sawn like so much wood or stone. And yet I felt no terror of death. I had been taken in a sleigh from the station to the hospital, over a mile or more of snow, and the one thought that worried me most, when I was supposed to be face to face with death, was whether the town lay north, south, east or west from the hospital; and this, I believe, was the last question I asked. After hearing the answer, I drew in the chloroform in long breaths, thinking to assist the doctors in their work. In spite of this, I have a faint recollection of struggling with all my might against its effects, previous to losing consciousness; but I was greatly surprised on being told afterwards that I had, when in that condition, used more foul language in ten minutes delirium than had probably been used in twenty-four hours by the whole population of Canada.

Autobiography of a Super-Tramp, 1908.

James Boswell

I GOT up excellently well. My present life is most curious, and very fortunately is become agreeable. My affairs are conducted with the greatest regularity and exactness, I move like clockwork. At eight in the morning, Molly lights the fire, sweeps and dresses my dining-room. Then she calls me up and lets me know what o'clock it is. I lie some time in bed indulging indolence, which in that way, when the mind is easy and cheerful, is most pleasing. I then slip on my clothes loosely, easily, and quickly, and come into my dining-room. I pull my bell. The maid lays a milk-white napkin upon the table and sets the things for breakfast. I then take some light amusing book and breakfast and read for an hour or more, gently pleasing both my palate and my mental taste. Breakfast over, I feel myself gay and lively. I go to the window and am entertained with the people passing by, all intent on different schemes. To go regularly through the day would be too formal for this my journal. Besides, every day cannot be passed in exactly the same way in every particular. My day is, in general diversified with reading of different kinds, playing on the violin, writing, chatting with my friends. Even the taking of medicines serves to make time go with less heaviness. I have a sort of genius for physic and always had great entertainment in observing the changes of the human body and the effects produced by diet, labour, rest, and physical operations. . . .

As I am now in tolerable health, my appetite is very good,

and I eat my slender bit of dinner with great relish. I drink a great deal of tea. Between eleven and twelve my bed is warmed and I go calmly to repose. I am not at all unsatisfied with this kind of existence. It is passing my portion of time very comfortably. Most philosophically do I reason upon this subject, being certainly the most important one to me at present. I consider that though I want many pleasures which are to be had by being abroad, yet also I want many pains. I am troubled by no dirty streets nor no jostling chairmen. Multitudes of ideas float through my fancy on both sides of the question. I shall now and then put some of them down as they strike me strongly.

I have now made a very near calculation of my expenses for the year, and found that I would be able to save £50 out of my allowance. This sum would be requisite for immediate necessaries in case of my getting a commission in the Guards, and I would have a pride to furnish it without any extraordinary assistance from my father, which it is reasonable he should allow in that event, as everybody thinks he should rig me out. However, if I can do without him, I must be called an excellent manager. Not satisfied with saving £50, I went to work still nearer, wishing to save £20 more, and with great thought and assiduity did I compute. In short, I found myself turning very fond of money and ruminating with a kind of transport on the idea of being worth £70 at the year's end. The desire of being esteemed a clever economist was no doubt mixed with it, but I seriously think that sheer love of coin was my predominant principle.

While I was strongly possessed with this inclination, my landlord came to wait on me, and renewed a proposal which he had formerly mentioned; and that was that if I would give up one of my rooms, there should be a reasonable abatement made of my rent. He said that a Mr Smith, a gentleman of good fortune, with his lady and son, wanted to take three rooms. I told him that I should be glad to do what was convenient for him and at the same time of advantage to myself; and that I considered my having two rooms above was unnecessary, as I had the parlour below to entertain my company in. I therefore agreed to the proposal, and he agreed to have a handsome tent-bed with green and white check curtains put up in the room to the street. By this means I can save several pounds a year. The thing happened most opportunely, while I was so much en-amoured of the money-making scheme. It gratified my passion while it was strong, which is quite the nice requisite for pleasure. A drink when a man is dry is highly relished. And in other gratifications, the analogy is good. But it must be observed that a great share of anxiety is the constant concomitant of this passion, so that the mind is as much hurt in one way as it is pleased in another. I felt this now very plainly. For while I hugged myself with the prospect of my golden possessions, I was in pain lest I should not be able to fulfil my conjecture, and had disagreeable struggles between the love of many amusing schemes that gaily started up to my imagination and my principal scheme of saving.

It is a good deal diverting to consider my present views. A young fellow of life and spirit, with an allowance extremely moderate, in so much that most people declare it must be wonderful management that can make it support a genteel existence, yet is this fellow gravely laying down plans for making rich and being a man of wealth. The love of property is strongly implanted in mankind. Property, to be sure, gives us a power of enjoying many pleasures which it can purchase; and as society is constituted, a man has a high degree of respect from it. Let me, however, beware of allowing this passion to take a deep root. It may engross my affections and give me a meanness of spirit and a cold indifference to every manly and spirited pursuit. And when we consider what one gains, it is merely imaginary. To keep the golden mean between stinginess and prodigality is the point I should aim at. If a man is prodigal, he cannot be truly generous. His money is foolishly dissipated, without any goodness on his part, and he has nothing to be generous with. On the other hand, a narrow man has a hard, contracted soul. The finer feelings are bound up, and although he has the power, he can never have the will to be generous.

The character worthy of imitation is the man of economy, who with prudent attention knows when to save and when to spend, and acts accordingly. Let me pursue this system. I have done so hitherto since my setting out upon my own footing. Let me continue it. Let me lay out my money with ease and freedom, though with judgment and caution; and if at the years end I should have a genteel sum remaining as a reward of my economy, let me congratulate myself on my felicity.

Upon my word, my journal goes on charmingly at present. I was very apprehensive that there would be a dreary vacancy in it for some weeks, but by various happy circumstances I have been agreeably disappointed. I think, too, that I am making good use of the hint which Captain Erskine gave me, and consequently writing it in a more correct style. Style is to sentiment what dress is to the person. The effects of both are very great, and both are acquired and improved by habit. When once we are used to it, it is as easy to dress neatly as like a sloven; in the same way, custom makes us write in a correct style as easily as in a careless, inaccurate one.

From his journal, February 9th, 1763.

Samuel Pepys

To my accounts of the whole year till past twelve at night, it being bitter cold, but yet I was well satisfied with my work; and, above all, to find myself, by the great blessing of God, worth £1349, by which, as I have spent very largely, so I have laid up above £500 this year above what I was worth this day twelvemonth. The Lord make me for ever thankful to his holy name for it! Soon as ever the clock struck one, I kissed my wife in the kitchen by the fire-side, wishing her a merry new year.

So ends the old year, I bless God, with great joy to me, not only for my having made so good a year of profit, as having spent £420 and laid up £540 and upwards; but I bless God I have never been in so good plight as to my health in so very cold weather as this is, nor indeed in any hot weather, these ten years, as I am at this day, and have been these four or five months. But I am at a great loss to know whether it be my hare's foot, or taking every morning a pill of turpentine, or my having left off the wearing of a gown. My family is my wife, in good health, and happy with her; her woman Mercer, a pretty, modest, quiet maid; her chamber-maid Bess, her cook-maid Jane, the little girl Susan, and my boy, which I have had about half a year, which I took from the King's Chapel; and a pretty and loving quiet family I have as any man in England. My credit in the world and my office grows daily, and I am in good esteem with everybody, I think. My troubles of my uncle's estate pretty well over; but it comes to be of little profit to us, my father being much supported by my purse. But great vexations remain upon my father and me from my brother Tom's death and ill condition, both to our disgrace and discontent, though no great reason for either. Public matters are all in a hurry about a Dutch war. Our preparations great; our provocations against them great; and, after all our presumption, we are now afraid as much of them as we lately contemned them. Everything else in the State quiet, blessed be God! My lord Sandwich at sea with the fleet at Portsmouth; sending some about to cruise for taking of ships, which we have done to a great number. This Christmas I judged it fit to look over all my papers and books, and to tear all that I found either boyish, or not to be worth keeping, or fit to be seen, if it should please God to take me suddenly. . . .

From his diary, December 31st, 1664.

Afflicted and Distressed

───────────⊙───────────

JOHN STUART MILL

WILLIAM COWPER

J. BLANCO WHITE

JANE WELSH CARLYLE

THOMAS CARLYLE

ARTHUR YOUNG

HENRY FYNES-CLINTON

MATTHIAS JOYCE

THOMAS DE QUINCEY

DENTON WELCH

W. N. P. BARBELLION

WILLIAM HAZLITT

MARGERY KEMPE

JOHN BUNYAN

GEORGE HERBERT

J. H. NEWMAN

John Stuart Mill

FROM the winter of 1821, when I first read Bentham, and especially from the commencement of the *Westminster Review*, I had what might truly be called an object in life; to be a reformer of the world. My conception of my own happiness was entirely identified with this object. The personal sympathies I wished for were those of fellow labourers in this enterprise. I endeavoured to pick up as many flowers as I could by the way; but as a serious and permanent personal satisfaction to rest upon, my whole reliance was placed on this; and I was accustomed to felicitate myself on the certainty of a happy life which I enjoyed, through placing my happiness in something durable and distant, in which some progress might be always making, while it could never be exhausted by complete attainment. This did very well for several years, during which the general improvement going on in the world and the idea of myself as engaged with others in struggling to promote it, seemed enough to fill up an interesting and animated existence. But the time came when I awakened from this as from a dream. It was in the autumn of 1826. I was in a dull state of nerves, such as everybody is occasionally liable to; unsusceptible to enjoyment or pleasurable excitement; one of those moods when what is pleasure at other times, becomes insipid or indifferent; the state, I should think, in which converts to Methodism usually are, when smitten by their first "conviction of sin." In this frame of mind it occurred to me to put the question directly to myself: "Suppose that all your objects in life were realised; that all the changes in institutions and opinions which you are looking forward to, could be completely effected at this very instant; would this be a great joy and happiness to you?" And an irrepressible self-consciousness distinctly answered, "No!" At this my heart sank within me: the whole foundation on which my life was constructed fell down. All my happiness was to have been found in the continual pursuit of this end. The end had ceased to charm, and how could there ever again be any interest in the means? I seemed to have nothing left to live for.

At first I hoped that the cloud would pass away of itself; but it did not. A night's sleep, the sovereign remedy for the smaller vexations of life, had no effect on it. I awoke to a renewed consciousness of the woeful fact. I carried it with me into all companies, into all occupations. Hardly anything had power to cause me even a few minutes' oblivion of it. For some months the cloud seemed to grow thicker and thicker. . . .

In vain I sought relief from my favourite books; those memorials of past nobleness and greatness from which I had always hitherto drawn strength and animation. I read them now without feeling, or with the accustomed feeling minus all its charm; and I became persuaded that my love of mankind, and of excellence for its own sake, had worn itself out. I sought no comfort by speaking to others of what I felt. If I had loved any-one sufficiently to make confiding my griefs a necessity, I should not have been in the condition I was. I felt, too, that mine was not an interesting, or in any way respectable distress. There was nothing in it to attract sympathy. Advice, if I had known where to seek it, would have been most precious. The words of Macbeth to the physician often occurred to my thoughts. But there was no one on whom I could build the faintest hope of such assistance. My father, to whom it would have been natural to me to have recourse in any practical difficulties, was the last person to whom, in such a case as this, I looked for help. Everything convinced me that he had no knowledge of any such mental state as I was suffering from, and that even if he could be made to understand it, he was not the physician who could heal it. My education, which was wholly his work, had been conducted without any regard to the possibility of its ending in this result; and I saw no use in giving him the pain of thinking that his plans had failed, when the failure was probably irremediable, and at all events beyond the power of *his* remedies. Of other friends, I had at that time none to whom I had any hope of making my condition intelligible. It was however abundantly intelligible to myself; and the more I dwelt upon it the more hopeless it appeared. . . . For I now saw, or thought I saw, what I had always before received with incredulity—that the habit of analysis has a tendency to wear away the feelings; as indeed it has, when no other mental habit is cultivated, and the analysing spirit remains without its natural complements and correctives.

An Autobiography, 1873.

William Cowper

I was bid to expect an examination at the bar of the House, touching my sufficiency for the post I had taken. Being necessarily ignorant of the nature of that business, it became expedient that I should visit the office daily, in order to qualify myself for the strictest scrutiny. All the horrors of my fears and perplexities now returned. A thunderbolt would have been as welcome to me as this intelligence. I knew, to demonstration, that upon these terms, the clerkship of the journals was no place for me. To require my attendance at the bar of the House, that I might there publicly entitle myself to the office was, in effect, to exclude me from it. In the mean time, the interest of my friend, the honor of his choice, my own reputation and circumstance, all urged me forward; all pressed me to undertake that which I saw to be impracticable. They whose spirits are formed like mine, to whom a public exhibition of themselves, on any occasion, is mortal poison, may have some idea of the horrors of my situation; others can have none.

My continual misery at length brought on a nervous fever:

quiet forsook me by day and peace by night; a finger raised against me, was more than I could stand against. In this posture of mind, I attended regularly at the office; where, instead of a soul upon the rack, the most active spirits were essentially necessary for my purpose. I expected no assistance from anybody there, all the inferior clerks being under the influence of my opponent; and accordingly I received none. The journal books were indeed thrown open to me; a thing which could not be refused; and from which, perhaps, a man in health, and with a head turned to business, might have gained all the information he wanted; but it was not so with me. I read without perception, and was so distressed, that had every clerk in the office been my friend, it could have availed me little; for I was not in a condition to receive instruction, far less to elicit it out of manuscripts, without direction. Many months went over me thus employed, constant in the use of means, despairing as to the issue. . . .

I now began to look upon madness as the only chance remaining. I had a strong kind of foreboding, that so it would one day fare with me; and I wished for it earnestly, and looked forward to it with impatient expectation. My chief fear was, that my senses would not fail in time enough to excuse my appearance at the bar of the House of Lords, which was the only purpose I wanted it to answer. Accordingly the day of decision drew nearer, and I was still in my senses; though in my heart I had formed many wishes, and by word of mouth expressed many expectations to the contrary.

Now came the grand temptation; the point to which Satan had all the while been driving me; the dark and hellish purpose of self-murder. I grew more sullen and reserved, fled from all society, even from my most intimate friends, and shut myself up in my chambers. The ruin of my fortune, the contempt of my relatives and acquaintances, the prejudice I should do my patron, were all urged upon me with irresistible energy. Being reconciled to the apprehension of madness, I began to be reconciled to the apprehension of death.

Memoir of the Early Life of William Cowper, Esq., 1816.

J. Blanco White

I HAVE taken a room in Duke Street, St James's, according to the plan I proposed to Lord and Lady H(olland). My absolute unfitness for the common dealings of life is very painful to me, but no previous resolution of mine is enought to prevent the silly awkwardness that seizes me as soon as I enter on business in which I have to contend with the interest of another. My excellent father was as unfit for making a bargain as myself. Whether such dispositions are hereditary, or whether (as I believe) the early impressions produced by domestic example transmit them from father to son, is a question which I will not stop to discuss. I have, however, to lament that a ridiculous delicacy for the feelings of people who have no claim to it, as being in all probability perfect strangers to the impression I am anxious to spare them, makes me a most helpless man in the daily business of life. This morning, for instance, I offered a guinea a week for the room which I am persuaded I might have had for fifteen shillings. The woman who lets it, a mean, sluttish old creature, asked for some money in advance as a security, though I had given her my address; but I had not the courage to ask for a receipt. It would be endless to enumerate the blunders of this kind which I make on similar occasions. I am seized with a shyness and confusion which could hardly be pardoned in a child. . .

It is indeed unquestionable that I have been, all my life, a most unfit person to manage money matters. But at this time, and during the long period when my internal complaint was increasing, my nervous timidity was extremely painful, and almost unmanageable. I remember the desperate effort which I was obliged to make before I ventured to knock at a door, and enquire whether the person I wanted to see was at home. Any sudden question upon the most simple or indifferent matter used to startle me, and put me into a state of trepidation which deprived me for some time of all the knowledge I might possess upon the subject. I believe that during that period, and at various times when, even in the course of my partial recovery, I have had some return of those symptoms, I must have given the most absurd answers, and often appeared to those who knew little or nothing of me, grossly ignorant. I remember instances of this at Oxford, especially in the Oriel Common Room. I do not know whether from modesty or from pride, whenever I have found myself in these situations, I have never made any attempt to correct the blunder, or to explain the cause of it. I have quietly submitted, most probably from a well grounded fear that I might get into a worse confusion; and from a sense of degradation which I have in connection with a self-defence upon such trifles. If those present will not explain the fact to themselves, I prefer leaving them under their mistake.

From his journal of February 1817.

Jane Welsh Carlyle

So many talents are wasted, so many enthusiasms turned to smoke, so many lives blighted for want of a little patience and endurance, for want of understanding and laying to heart that which you have so well expressed in these verses—the meaning of *the Present*—for want of recognising that it is not the greatness or littleness of "the duty nearest hand", but the spirit in which one does it, that makes one's doing noble or mean!

I can't think how people who have any natural ambition, and any sense of power in them, escape going *mad* in a world like this, without the recognition of that! I know I was very near mad when I found it out for myself (as one has to find out for oneself everything that is to be of any real practical use to one). Shall I tell you how it came into my head? Perhaps it may be of comfort to you in similar moments of fatigue and disgust.

I had gone with my husband to live on a little estate of *peat bog*, that had descended to me, all the way down from John Welsh the Covenanter, who married a daughter of John Knox. *That* didn't, I'm ashamed to say, make me feel Craigenputtock a whit less of a peat bog, and most dreary, untoward place to live at. In fact, it was sixteen miles distant on every side from all the conveniences of life—shops, and even post office!

Further, we were very *poor*, and, further and worst, being an only child, and brought up to "great prospects", I was sublimely ignorant of every branch of useful knowledge, though a capital Latin scholar and a very fair mathematician!! It behoved me in these astonishing circumstances to learn—to sew! Husbands, I was shocked to find, wore their stockings into holes! and were always losing buttons! and *I* was expected to "look to all that". Also, it behoved me to learn *to cook*! No capable servant choosing to live at "such an out of the way place", and my husband having "bad digestion", which complicated my difficulties dreadfully. The bread above all, brought from Dumfries, "soured on his stomach" (oh Heavens!); and it was plainly my duty as a Christian wife to bake at home! So I sent for Cobbett's *Cottage Economy*, and fell to work at a loaf of bread. But knowing nothing of the process of fermentation or the heat of ovens, it came to pass that my loaf got put into the oven at the time myself ought to have put to bed, and I remained the only person not asleep, in a house in the middle of a desert! One o'clock struck, and then two and then three; and still I was sitting there in an intense solitude, my whole body aching with weariness, my heart aching with a sense of forlornness and *degredation*. "That I who had been so petted at home, whose comfort had been studied by everybody in the house, who had never been required to *do* anything but *cultivate my mind*, should have to pass all those hours of the night watching *a loaf of bread*! which mightn't turn out bread after all!"

Such thoughts maddened me, till I laid my head on the table and sobbed aloud. It was then that somehow the idea of Benvenuto Cellini's sitting up all night watching his Perseus in the oven came into my head; and suddenly I asked myself, "After all, in the sight of the upper powers, what is the mighty difference between a statue of Perseus and a loaf of bread, so that each be the thing one's hand hath found to do? The man's determined will, his energy, his patience, his resource, were the really admirable things, of which the statue of Perseus was the mere chance expression. If he had been a woman living at Craigenputtock, with a dyspeptic husband, sixteen miles from a baker, *and he a bad one*, all these same qualities would have come out most fitting in a *good* loaf of bread!"

I cannot express what consolation this germ of an idea spread over an uncongenial life, during the five years we lived at that savage place; where my two immediate predecessors had gone *mad*, and the third had taken to *drink*.

A letter to Miss Mary Smith, January 11th, 1857.

Thomas Carlyle

HER arrival (in London) I best of all remember; ah me! She was clear for *this* poor house (which she gradually, as poverty a little withdrew after long years of pushing, has made so beautiful and comfortable) in preference to all my other samples: and *here* we spent our two-and thirty years of hard battle against Fate; hard but not quite unvictorious, when she left me, as in her car of heaven's fire. My noble one! I say deliberately *her* part in the stern battle, and except myself none knows how stern, was brighter, and braver than my own. Thanks, Darling, for your shining words and acts, which were continual in my eyes, and in no other mortal's. Worthless I was your divinity; wrapt in your perpetual love of me and pride in me, in defiance of all men and things. Oh was it not beautiful, all this that I have lost for ever! And I was Thomas the *Doubter*, the Unhoping; till now only Half-believing, in myself and my priceless opulences!— At my return from Annandale, after *French Revolution*, she so cheerily recounted to me all the good "items", item after item, "Oh, it has had a great success, Dear!"—to no purpose, and at length beautifully lost patience with me for my incredulous humour. My life has not wanted at any time what I used to call *"desperate* hope" to all lengths; but of common *"hoping* hope" it has had but little; and has been shrouded since youthhood (almost since boyhood, for my school-years, at Annan, were very miserable, harsh, barren and worse) in continual gloom and grimness, as of a man set too nakedly versus the Devil and all men. Could I be easy to live with? She flickered round me, like perpetual radiance; and in spite of my glooms and my misdoings would at no moment cease to love me and help me. What of bounty too is in heaven!

Reminiscences of Thomas Carlyle, 1881.

Arthur Young

MY poor child breathed her last at twelve minutes past one o'clock on Friday morning the 14th (of July). I was on my knees at her bedside in great agony of mind. She looked at me and said, "Pray for me." I assured her that I did. She replied, "Do it now, papa," on which I poured forth aloud ejaculations to the Almighty that He would have compassion and heal the affliction of my child. She clasped her hands together in the attitude of praying, and when I had done said "Amen"—her last words.

Thank God of His infinite mercy she expired without a groan, or her face being the least agitated; her inspirations were gradually changed from being very distressing, till they became lost in gentleness, and at the last she went off like a bird.

Thus fled one of the sweetest tempers and, for her years, one of the best understandings that I ever met with. She was a companion for mature years, for there was in her none of the childish stuff of most girls. And thus fled the first hope of my life, the child on which I wished to rest in the affliction of my age. But the Almighty's will be done, and may I turn the event to the benefit of my soul, and in such a manner as to trust through the mediation of my Redeemer to become worthy to join her in a better world. . . .

I determined that her remains should be carried to Bradfield, having a warm hope of being animated to a more fervent devotion by the idea of her ashes being deposited in our own village church. To the departed spirit it is less than nothing—to me it may do good, and I have need of working out my salvation with fear and trembling. I feel that a wretched and depressed state of mind leads me to more Christian thoughts and more favourable to religious impressions than prosperity, or ease, or happiness, as it is called, and therefore hope I am justified in doing it; and if my family think the same, they also will derive benefit. . . .

On Monday the 17th I arrived at Bradfield, where every object is full of the dear deceased.

On going into the library the window looks into the little garden where I have so many times seen her happy. O gracious and merciful God! pardon me for allowing any earthly object thus to engross my feelings and overpower my whole soul! But what were they not on seeing and weeping over the roses, variegated sage and other plants she had set there and cultivated with her own dear hands. But every room, every spot is full of her, and it sinks my very heart to see them.

Tuesday evening, the 18th, her remains arrived, and at midnight her brother read the service over her in a most impressive manner. I buried her in my pew, fixing the coffin so that when I kneel it will be between her head and her dear heart. This I did as a means of preserving the grief I feel, and hope to feel while breath is in my body. It turns all my views to an hereafter, and fills my mind with earnest wishes, that when the great Author of my existence may please to take me, I may join my child in a better world.

From his journal of July, 1787.

H. Fynes-Clinton

AMONG the disadvantages under which I laboured, in this early period of my bereavement, I may reckon the want of a due sense of the duty and necessity of submission to the Divine will. Another disadvantage was the injudicious kindness of my friends, who endeavoured to obliterate in my mind the sense of my calamity by urging me to forget it, and by making haste to forget it themselves. This deportment irritated my feelings exceedingly. I felt that the memory of the departed was injuriously treated, and I determined, in a spirit of indignation, to persevere in my sorrow, and to magnify to my own imagination the greatness of my misfortune.

The most solid advantage which I possessed at this period, and the most effectual resource, was the love of reading, and the faculty of creating for myself an interest in the objects of literary pursuit. Literary occupation, useful to all men, under all circumstances, for the purposes of discipline and improvement, is most especially beneficial to him who labours under some severe misfortune, by relieving him from the greatest of all possible dangers, the want of occupation. From this perilous condition I was rescued by my love of study; to which I applied myself with an ardour that even bodily indisposition did not subdue.

AFFLICTED AND DISTRESSED

Returning in these six months to my classical studies, I laid the foundation of that habit of literary application which has since remained with me, and from which I have reaped the most important advantages.

Literary Remains, 1854.

Matthias Joyce

WHEN I was enabled to turn my face towards Zion, I endeavoured to give all my diligence to escape the wrath to come. To this end I not only denied myself of all ungodliness and worldly lusts, but, in some instances, even of that which was lawful. It was common for me to fast twenty-four hours at a time, and once, from Thursday night till Saturday morning. Add to this, my eagerness to redeem my time, so that I could hardly bear the thoughts of going to bed. I have stood reading and writing, in the winter season, sometimes till two o'clock in the morning, till the calves of my legs were quite numbed with cold; and scarcely ever did I go to bed, until so conquered by sleep that the book dropped out of my hand. But though I was last in bed, I was generally the first up; so that I seldom got more than four hours sleep. Five o'clock in the morning seldom catched me upon my pillow; for as I went to bed with reluctance, I stayed in it as short time as I could. And whatever time I was up before preaching, I employed either upon my knees, or in the Bible, or in some other good book: add to these, hard labour in my business, deep thinking, fierce temptations, and a wounded spirit! All these together bore heavily upon my constitution, and so impaired my health, that I was filled with wind, and contracted a bad digestion to such a degree, that the food I took, merely to support nature, lay like lead upon my stomach. At last I became burdensome to myself, and was distressed above measure.

176

But Satan, who always watches his opportunity to deceive the simple, took advantage, and suggested that I was a glutton, or I would not be so oppressed with my food. As I believed him, though I took care to eat moderately, and sometimes would not eat at all, I frequently concluded that my belly would destroy my soul. On this account I have often stretched myself upon the floor, and twisted and twined in pain, crying to the Lord for deliverance. One thing I remarked, that the Sabbath-day was the day of sorest trial to me; so that I have denied myself of all food the most part of that day, endeavouring, if possible, to worship God in spirit and in truth.

For nearly two years, I was oppressed in this manner. And though I had frequent manifestations of the goodness of God, and could at times rejoice exceedingly in his salvation, yet it was, in many respects, a dark and cloudy day.

The Life of Mr Matthias Joyce, included in *Lives of the Early Methodist Preachers, chiefly written by themselves,* 1837.

Thomas De Quincey

MY studies have now been long interrupted. I cannot read to myself with any pleasure, hardly with a moment's endurance. Yet I sometimes read aloud for the pleasure of others; because reading is an accomplishment of mine, and, in the slang use of the word *accomplishment* as a superficial and ornamental attainment, almost the only one I possess; and formerly, if I had any vanity at all connected with any endowment or attainment of mine, it was with this; for I had observed that no accomplishment is more rare. . . .

For nearly two years I believe that I read nothing and studied nothing. Analytic studies are continuous studies, and not to be pursued by fits and starts, or fragmentary efforts. All these were become insupportable to me; I shrank from them with a sense of powerless and infantine feebleness that gave me an anguish the greater from remembering the time when I grappled with them to my own hourly delight; and for this further reason, because I had devoted the labour of my whole life, had dedicated my intellect, blossoms and fruits, to the slow and elaborate toil of constructing one single work, to which I had presumed to give the title of an unfinished work of Spinosa's—viz. *De Emendatione Humani Intellectus.* This was now lying locked up as by frost, like any Spanish bridge or acqueduct begun upon too great a scale for the resources of the architect; and, instead of surviving me, as a monument of wishes at least, and aspirations, and long labours, dedicated to the exaltation of human nature in that way in which God had best fitted me to promote so great an object, it was likely to stand a memorial to my children of hopes defeated, of baffled efforts, of materials uselessly accumulated, of foundations laid that were never to support a superstructure, of the grief and the ruin of the architect. In this state of imbecility, I had, for amusement, turned my attention to political economy. My understanding, which formerly had been as active and restless as a panther, could not, I suppose, (so long as I lived at all), sink into utter lethargy; and political economy offers this advantage to a person in my state,—that, though it is eminently an organic science (no part, that is to say, but what acts on the whole, as the whole again reacts on and through each part), yet still the several parts may be detached and contemplated singly. Great as was the prostration of my powers at this time, yet I could not forget my knowledge; and my understanding had been for too many years intimate with severe thinkers, with logic, and the great masters of knowledge, not to be aware of a great call made by political economy at this crisis for a new law and a transcendent legislator. Suddenly, in 1818, a friend in Edinburgh sent me down Mr Ricardo's book; and, recurring to my own prophetic anticipation of some coming legislator for this science, I said, before I had finished the first chapter, "Thou art the man!" Wonder and curiosity were emotions that had long been dead in me. Yet I wondered once more—wondered at myself that could once again be stimulated to the effort of reading; and much more I wondered at the book. Had this profound work been really written during the tumultuous hurry of the nineteenth century? Could it be that an Englishman, and he not in academic bowers, but oppressed by mercantile and senatorial cares, had accomplished what all the universities of Europe, and a century of thought, had failed even to advance by one hair's-breadth? Previous writers had been crushed and overlaid by the enormous weights of facts, details and exceptions; Mr Ricardo had deduced, *a priori*, from the understanding itself, laws which first shot arrowy light into the dark chaos of materials, and had thus constructed what hitherto was but a collection of tentative discussions into a science of regular proportions, now first standing upon an eternal basis.

Thus did one simple work of a profound understanding avail to give me a pleasure and an activity which I had not known for years; it roused me even to write, or, at least, to dictate what M. – wrote for me. It seemed to me that some important truths had escaped even the "inevitable eye" of Mr Ricardo; and, as these were, for the most part, of such a nature that I could express or illustrate them briefly and elegantly by algebraic symbols, the whole would hardly have reached the bulk of a pamphlet. With M.– for my amanuensis, even at this time, incapable as I was of all general exertion, I drew up, therefore, my "Prolegomena to all Future Systems of Political Economy."

The exertion, however, was but a momentary flash, as the sequel showed. Arrangements were made at a provincial press, about eighteen miles distant, for printing it. An additional compositor was retained for some days on this account. The work was even twice advertised; and I was, in a manner, pledged to the fulfilment of my intention. But I had a preface to write, and a dedication, which I wished to make impressive, to Mr Ricardo. I found myself quite unable to accomplish all this. The arrangements were countermanded, the compositor dismissed, and my "Prolegomena" rested peacefully by the side of its elder and more dignified brother.

In thus describing and illustrating my intellectual torpor, I use terms that apply, more or less, to every part of the years during which I was under the Circean spells of opium. But for misery and suffering, I might, indeed, be said to have existed in a dormant state. I seldom could prevail on myself to write a letter; an answer of a few words to any that I received, was the utmost that I could accomplish; and often *that* not until the letter had lain for weeks, or even months, upon my writing-table. Without the aid of M.—, my whole domestic economy, whatever became of political economy, must have gone into irretrievable confusion. I shall not afterwards allude to this part of the case; it is one, however, which the opium-eater will find, in the end, most oppressive and tormenting, from the sense of incapacity and feebleness, from the direct embarrassments incident to the neglect or procrastination of each day's appropriate labours, and from the remorse which must often exasperate the stings of these evils to a conscientious mind. The opium-eater loses none of his moral sensibilities or aspirations; he wishes and longs as earnestly as ever to realise what he believes possible, and feels to be exacted by duty; but his intellectual apprehension of what is possible infinitely outruns his power, not of execution only, but even of proposing or willing. He lies under a world's weight of incubus and nightmare; he lies in sight of all that he would fain perform, just as a man forcibly confined to his bed by the mortal languor of paralysis, who is compelled to witness injury or outrage to some object of his tenderest love—he would lay down his life if he might but rise and walk; but he is powerless as an infant, and cannot so much as make an effort to move.

Confessions of an English Opium Eater. Revised edition, 1856.

Denton Welch

As I lie in bed here, now, this morning, and watch the crystal glittering of the candlesticks, the white iron twisting table, the yellow satin chair, the grey morning light on the crusty bark of the trees; as I watch the patiently silent harpsichord and the scarlet lacquer screen behind it, and the four miniatures of people long since dead; I think of myself as dead. I think of the years and years to come, when the sun will rise and I shall be nothing but a burnt up cinder. I think of myself as two eyes looking down on my empty room, on my silent velvet bed, on all my pretty things, and knowing that I shall never use them again. I think of them floating into other people's homes and being used a hundred years from hence. I think of wars and torture and the blackest sins of power. I think of babies and all the screaming life of eternity.

This is the horrible, beautiful immortality that we've been looking for. The never-ending of our race on earth. How it pierces down and seems to light everything with a lurid glow— this knowledge of what is in store. And all the ideas of behaviour of Jane Austen and our own, all our delightful and nasty little snobbisms and aspirations, all our fears of offending— how exciting, how sad and heart-rending they become when we think of them under the heavy layers of dust and earth, under the dripping trees in the church-yard, under the down-pressing sagging-with-rain sky. O think of feather boas and reticules and white kid gloves that have been buried for a hundred years.

From his journal, February 12th, 1945.

W. N. P. Barbellion

I SUFFER from such a savage *amour propre* that I fear to enter the lists with a man I dislike on account of the mental anguish I should suffer if he worsted me. I am therefore bottled up tight—both my hates and loves. For a coward is not only afraid to tell a man he hates him, but is nervous too of letting go his feeling of affection or regard lest it be rejected or not returned. I shudder to think of such remarks as (referring to me), "He's one of my admirers, you know" (sardonically), or "I simply can't get rid of him."

If however my cork *does* come out, there is an explosion, and placid people occasionally marvel to hear violent language streaming from my lips and nasty acid and facetious remarks.

Of course, to intimate friends (only about three persons in the wide, wide world), I can always give free vent to my feelings, and I do so in privacy with that violence in which a weak character usually finds some compensation for his intolerable self-imposed reserve and restraint in public. I can never marvel enough at the ineradicable turpitude of my existence, at my *double-facedness*, and at the remarkable contrast between the face I turn to the outside world and the face my friends know. It's like leading a double existence or artificially constructing a puppet to dangle before the crowd while I fulminate behind the scenes. If only I had the moral courage to play my part in life— to take the stage and be myself, to enjoy the delightful sensation of making my presence felt, instead of this vapourish mumming —then this Journal would be quite unnecessary. For to me self-expression is a necessity of life, and what cannot be expressed in one way must be expressed in another. When colossal egotism is driven underground, whether by a steely surface environment or an unworkable temperament or as in my case by both, you get a truly remarkable result, and the victim a truly remarkable pain—the pain one might say of continuously unsuccessful attempts at parturition.

The Journal of a Disappointed Man, 1919.

William Hazlitt

WHAT sometimes surprises me in looking back to the past is . . . to find myself so little changed in the time. The same images and trains of thought stick by me; I have the same tastes, likings, sentiments and wishes I had then. One source of this unbendingness (which some may call obstinacy) is that, though living much alone, I have never worshipped the Echo. I see plainly enough that black is not white, that the grass is green, that kings are not their subjects; and, in such self-evident cases, do not think it necessary to collate my opinions with the received prejudices. In subtler questions, and matters that admit of doubt, as I do not impose my opinion on others without a reason, so I will not give up mine to them without a better reason; and a person calling me names, or giving himself airs of authority, does not convince me of his having taken more pains to find out the truth than I have, but the contrary. . . .

Both from disposition and habit I can *assume* nothing, in word, look or manner. I cannot steal a march on public opinion in any way. My standing upright, speaking loud, entering a room gracefully, prove nothing; therefore I neglect these ordinary means of recommending myself to the good graces and admiration of strangers (and, as it appears, even of philosophers and friends). Why? Because I have other resources, or, at least, am absorbed in other studies and pursuits. Suppose this absorption to be extreme, and even morbid, that I have brooded over an idea till it has become a kind of substance in my brain, that I have reasons for a thing which I have found out with much labour and pain, and to which I can scarcely do justice without the utmost violence of exertion (and that only to a few persons)— is this a reason for my playing off my out-of-the-way notions in all companies, wearing a prim and complacent air, as if I were "the admired of all observers"? or is it not rather an argument (together with a want of animal spirits) why I should retire into myself, and perhaps acquire a nervous and uneasy look, from a consciousness of the disproportion between the interest and the conviction I feel on certain subjects, and my ability to communicate what weighs upon my own mind to others? If my ideas, which I do not avouch, but suppose, lie below the surface, why am I to be always attempting to dazzle superficial people with them, or smiling, delighted, at my own want of success?

Farewell to Essay-writing, 1828.

Margery Kempe

WHEN the time came that this creature should visit those holy places where our Lord was quick and dead, as she had by revelation years before, she prayed the parish priest of the town where she was dwelling, to say for her in the pulpit that, if any man or woman claimed any debt from her husband or herself, they should come and speak with her ere she went, and she, with the help of God, would make a settlement with each of them, so that they should hold themselves content. And so she did.

Afterwards she took leave of her husband and of the holy anchorite, who had told her, before, the process of her going and the great dis-ease that she would suffer by the way, and when all her fellowship forsook her, how a broken-backed man would lead her forth in safety, through the help of our Lord.

And so it befell indeed, as shall be written afterward.

Then she took leave of Master Robert, and prayed him for his blessing, and so, forth of other friends. Then she went forth to Norwich, and offered at the Trinity, and afterwards she went to Yarmouth and offered at an image of our Lady, and there she took her ship.

And next day they came to a great town called Zierikzee, where our Lord of His high goodness visited this creature with abundant tears of contrition for her own sins, and sometime for other men's sins also. And especially she had tears of compassion in mind of our Lord's Passion. And she was houselled each Sunday where there was time and place convenient thereto, with great weeping and boisterous sobbing, so that many men marvelled and wondered at the great grace that God had wrought in His creature.

This creature had eaten no flesh and drunk no wine for four years ere she went out of England, and so now her ghostly father charged her, by virtue of obedience, that she should both eat flesh and drink wine. And so she did a little while; afterwards she prayed her confessor that he would hold her excused if she ate no flesh, and suffer her to do as she would for such time as pleased him.

And soon after, through the moving of some of her company, her confessor was displeased because she ate no flesh, and so were many of the company. And they were most displeased because she wept so much and spoke always of the love and goodness of Our Lord, as much at the table as in other places. And therefore shamefully they reproved her, and severely chid her, and said they would not put up with her as her husband did when she was at home and in England.

And she answered meekly to them: "Our Lord, Almighty God, is as great a Lord here as in England, and as good cause have I to love Him here as there, blessed may He be."

At these words her fellowship was angrier than before, and

their wrath and unkindness to this creature was a matter of great grief, for they were held right good men and she desired greatly their love, if she might have it to the pleasure of God.

And then she said to one of them specially: "Ye cause me much shame and great grievance."

He answered her anon:—"I pray God that the devil's death may overcome thee soon and quickly", and many more cruel words he said to her than she could repeat.

And soon after some of the company in whom she trusted best, and her own maiden also, said she could not longer go in their fellowship. And they said that they would take away her maiden from her, so that she should no strumpet be, in her company. And then one of them, who had her gold in keeping, left her a noble with great anger and vexation to go where she would and help herself as she might, for with them, they said, she should no longer abide; and they forsook her that night.

Then, on the next morning, there came to her one of their company, a man who loved her well, praying her that she would go to his fellows and meeken herself to them, and pray them that she might go still in their company till she came to Constance.

And so she did, and went forth with them till she came to Constance with great discomfort and great trouble, for they did her much shame and much reproof as they went, in divers places. They cut her gown so short that it came but little beneath her knee, and made her put on a white canvas, in the manner of a sacken apron, so that she should be held a fool and the people should not make much of her or hold her in repute. They made her sit at the table's end, below all the others, so that she ill durst speak a word.

And notwithstanding all their malice, she was held in more worship than they were, wherever they went.

And the good man of the house where they were hostelled, though she sat lowest at the table's end, would always help her before them all as well as he could, and sent her from his own table such service as he had, and that annoyed her fellowship full evil.

As they went by the way Constance-ward, it was told them that they would be robbed and have great discomfort unless they had great grace. Then this creature came to a church and went in to make her prayer, and she prayed with all her heart, with great weeping and many tears, for help and succour against their enemies.

The our Lord said to her mind:—"Dread thee naught, daughter, thy fellowship shall come to no harm whilst thou art in their company."

And so, blessed may our Lord be in all His works, they went forth in safety to Constance.

The Book of Margery Kempe. Modernised version, 1936.

John Bunyan

I WILL tell you a pretty business; I was once above all the rest in a very sad and low condition for many weeks; at which time also I, being but a young prisoner, and not acquainted with the laws, had this lay much upon my spirit, That my imprisonment might end at the gallows for aught that I could tell. Now, therefore, Satan laid hard at me to beat me out of heart, by suggesting this unto me, But how if when you come indeed to die, you should be in this condition; that is, as not to savour the things of God, not to have any evidence upon your soul for a better state hereafter? For indeed at that time all the things of God were hid from my soul.

Wherefore, when I at first began to think of this, it was a great trouble to me; for I thought with myself, that in the condition I now was in, I was not fit to die, neither indeed did I think I could, if I should be called to it: besides, I thought with myself, if I should make a scrabbling shift to clamber up the ladder, yet I should either with quaking, or other symptoms of faintings, give occasion to the enemy to reproach the way of God and his people, for their timorousness. This therefore lay with great trouble upon me, for methought I was ashamed to die with a pale face and tottering knees, for such a cause as this.

Wherefore, I prayed to God that he would comfort me, and give me strength to do and suffer what he should call me to; yet no comfort appeared, but all continued hid: I was also at this time so really possessed with the thought of death, that oft I was as if I was on the ladder with a rope about my neck; only this was some encouragement to me, I thought I might now have an opportunity to speak my last words to a multitude, which I thought would come to see me die; and, thought I, if it must be so, if God will but convert one soul by my very last words, I shall not count my life thrown away, nor lost.

But yet all the things of God were kept out of my sight, and still the tempter followed me with, But whither must you go when you die? What will become of you? Where will you be found in another world? What evidence have you for heaven and glory, and an inheritance among them that are sanctified? Thus was I tossed for many weeks, and knew not what to do; at last this consideration fell with weight upon me, That it was for the Word and way of God that I was in this condition, wherefore I was engaged not to flinch a hair's breadth from it.

I thought also, that God might choose whether he would give me comfort now or at the hour of death, but I might not therefore choose whether I would hold my profession or no; I was bound, but he was free: yea, it was my duty to stand to his word, whether he would ever look upon me or no, or save me at the last: wherefore, thought I, the point being thus, I am for going on, and venturing my eternal state with Christ, whether I have comfort here or no; if God doth not come in, thought I, I will leap off the ladder even blindfold into eternity, sink or swim, come heaven, come hell, Lord Jesus, if thou wilt catch me, do; if not, I will venture for thy name.

A Relation of the Imprisonment of Mr John Bunyan.

George Herbert

Affliction

When first thou didst entice to thee my heart
    I thought the service brave:
So many joys I writ down for my part,
    Besides what I might have
Out of my stock of natural delights
Augmented with thy gracious benefits.

I looked on thy furniture so fine,
    And made it fine to me:
Thy glorious household-stuff did me entwine,
    And 'tice me unto thee.
Such stars I counted mine: both heav'n and earth
Paid me my wages in a world of mirth.

What pleasures could I want, whose King I served,
    Where joys my fellows were?
Thus argued into hopes, my thoughts reserved
    No place for grief or fear.
Therefore my sudden soul caught at the place,
And made her youth and fierceness seek thy face.

At first thou gav'st me milk and sweetnesses;
    I had my wish and way:
My days were straw'd with flow'rs and happiness;
    There was no month but May.
But with my years sorrow did twist and grow,
And made a party unawares for woe.

My flesh began unto my soul in pain,
    Sicknesses cleave my bones;
Consuming agues dwell in ev'ry vein,
    And tune my breath to groans.
Sorrow was all my soul; I scarce believed,
Till grief did tell me roundly, that I lived.

When I got health, thou took'st away my life,
    And more; for my friends die:
My mirth and edge was lost; a blunted knife
    Was of more use than I.
Thus thin and lean without a fence or friend,
I was blown through with ev'ry storm and wind.

Whereas my birth and spirit rather took
    The way that takes the town,
Thou didst betray me to a ling'ring book,
    And wrap me in a gown.
I was entangled in the world of strife,
Before I had the power to change my life.

Yet, for I threaten'd oft the siege to raise,
    Not simp'ring all mine age,
Thou often didst with academic praise
    Melt and dissolve my rage.
I took thy sweeten'd pill, till I came where
I could not go away, nor persevere.

Yet lest perchance I should too happy be
    In my unhappiness,
Turning my purge to food, thou throwest me
    Into more sicknesses.
Thus doth thy power cross-bias me, not making
Thine own gift good, yet me from my ways taking.

Now I am here, what thou wilt do with me
    None of my books will show:
I read, and sigh, and wish I were a tree;
    For sure then I should grow
To fruit or shade: at least some bird would trust
Her household to me, and I should be just.

Yet, though thou troublest me, I must be meek;
    In weakness must be stout.
Well, I will change the service, and go seek
    Some other master out.
Ah, my dear God! though I am clean forgot,
Let me not love thee, if I love thee not.

The Temple, 1633.

J. H. Newman

AND now that I am about to trace, as far as I can, the course of
that great revolution of mind which led me to leave my own home,
to which I was bound by so many strong and tender ties, I feel
overcome with the difficulty of satisfying myself in my account
of it, and have recoiled from doing so, till the near approach of
the day, on which these lines must be given to the world, forces
me to set about the task. For who can know himself, and the
multitude of subtle influences which act upon him? and who can
recollect, at the distance of twenty-five years, all that he once
knew about his thoughts and his deeds, and that, during a portion
of his life, when even at the time his observation, whether of
himself or of the external world, was less than before or after,
by very reason of the perplexity and dismay which weighed
upon him, — when, though it would be most unthankful to seem to
imply that he had not all-sufficient light amid his darkness, yet a

darkness emphatically it was? And who can gird himself suddenly to a new and anxious undertaking, which he might be able indeed to perform well, had he full and calm leisure to look through every thing that he has written, whether in published works or private letters? But, on the other hand, as to that calm contemplation of the past, in itself so desirable, who can afford to be leisurely and deliberate, while he practises on himself a cruel operation, the ripping up of old griefs, and the venturing again upon the *infandum dolorem* of years, in which the stars of this lower heaven were one by one going out? I could not in cold blood, nor except upon the imperious call of duty, attempt what I have set myself to do. It is both to head and heart an extreme trial, thus to analyze what has so long gone by, and to bring out the results of that examination. I have done various bold things in my life: this is the boldest: and were I not sure I should after all succeed in my object, it would be madness to set about it.

Apologia pro Vita Sua, 1864.

Dedicated
Spirits

———————— ❦ ————————

WILLIAM BLAKE

P. B. SHELLEY

JOHN MILTON

GEORGE FOX

THOMAS ELLWOOD

W. B. YEATS

EDWIN MUIR

JOHN KEATS

RICHARD JEFFERIES

ERIC GILL

B. R. HAYDON

JOSEPH CONRAD

William Blake

You have so generously and openly desired that I will divide my griefs with you that I cannot hide what it is now become my duty to explain. My unhappiness has arisen from a source which, if explored too narrowly, might hurt my pecuniary circumstances, as my dependence is on engraving at present, and particularly on the engravings I have in hand for Mr H.; and I find on all hands great objections to my doing anything but the mere drudgery of business, and intimations that if I do not confine myself to this, I shall not live; this has always pursued me. You will understand by this the source of all my uneasiness. This from Johnson and Fuseli brought me down here, and this from Mr H. will bring me back again; for that I cannot live without doing my duty to lay up treasures in heaven is certain and determined, and to this I have long made up my mind, and why this should be made an objection to me, while drunkenness, lewdness, gluttony and even idleness itself does not hurt other men, let Satan himself explain. The thing I have most at heart—more than life, or all that seems to make life comfortable without—is the interest of true religion and science, and whenever anything appears to affect that interest (especially if I myself omit any duty to my station as a soldier of Christ), it gives me the greatest of torments. I am not ashamed, afraid, or averse to tell you what ought to be told: that I am under the direction of messengers from Heaven, daily and nightly; but the nature of such things is not, as some suppose, without trouble and care. Temptations are on the right hand and left; behind, the sea of time and space roars and follows swiftly; he who keeps not right onward is lost, and if our footsteps slide in clay, how can we do otherwise than fear and tremble? But I should not have troubled you with this account

195

of my spiritual state, unless it had been necessary in explaining the actual cause of my uneasiness, into which you are so kind as to enquire; for I never obtrude such things upon others unless questioned, and then I never disguise the truth. But if we fear to do the dictates of our Angels, and tremble at the tasks set before us; if we refuse to do spiritual acts because of natural fears or natural desires! Who can describe the dismal torments of such a state! I too well remember the threats I heard! "If you, who are organised by Divine Providence for spiritual communion, refuse, and bury your talent in the earth, even though you should want natural bread, sorrow and desperation pursues you thro' life, and after death shame and confusion of face to eternity. Every one in Eternity will leave you, aghast at the man who was crowned with glory and honour by his brethren, and betrayed their cause to their enemies. You will be called the base Judas who betrayed his Friend!" Such words would make any man tremble, and how then could I be at ease? But I am now no longer in that state, and now go on again with my task, fearless, and though my path is difficult, I have no fear of stumbling while I keep it.

A letter to Thomas Butts, January 10th, 1802.

P. B. Shelley

While yet a boy I sought for ghosts, and sped
   Through many a listening chamber, cave and ruin,
   And starlight wood, with fearful steps pursuing
Hopes of high talk with the departed dead.
I called on poisonous names with which our youth is fed;
   I was not heard—I saw them not—
   When musing deeply on the lot
Of life, at that sweet time when winds are wooing

All vital things that wake to bring
News of birds and blossoming,—
Sudden, thy shadow fell on me;
I shrieked, and clasped my hands in ecstasy!

I vowed that I would dedicate my powers
 To thee and thine—have I not kept the vow?
 With beating heart and streaming eyes, even now
I call the phantoms of a thousand hours
Each from his voiceless grave; they have in visioned bowers
 Of studious zeal or love's delight
 Outwatched with me the envious night—
They know that never joy illumed my brow
 Unlinked with hope that thou wouldst free
 This world from its dark slavery,
 That thou—O awful Loveliness,
Wouldst give whate'er these words cannot express.

   Stanzas from *A Hymn to Intellectual Beauty*, 1816.

John Milton

FOR although a poet, soaring in the high region of his fancies, with his garland and singing robes about him, might, without apology, speak more of himself than I mean to do; yet for me sitting here below in the cool element of prose, a mortal thing among many readers of no empyreal conceit, to venture and indulge unusual things of myself, I shall petition to the gentler sort, it may not be envy to me. I must say, therefore, that after I had from my first years, by the ceaseless diligence and care of my father (whom God recompense) been exercised to the tongues, and some sciences, as my age would suffer, by sundry masters and teachers, both at home and at the schools, it was found that whether aught was imposed me by them that had the overlooking, or betaken to of mine own choice, in English, or other tongue, prosing or versing, but chiefly this latter, the style, by certain vital signs it had, was likely to live. But much latelier, in the private academies of Italy, whither I was favoured to resort, perceiving that some trifles which I had in memory, composed at under twenty or thereabout (for the manner is, that every one must give some proof of his wit and reading there,) met with acceptance above what was looked for; and other things, which I had shifted in scarcity of books and conveniences to patch up amongst them, were received with written encomiums, which the Italian is not forward to bestow on men of this side of the Alps; I began thus far to assent both to them and divers of my friends here at home, and not less to an inward prompting which now grew daily upon me, that by labour and intent study (which I take to be my portion in this life), jointed with the strong propensity of nature, I might perhaps leave something so written to aftertimes, as they should not willingly let die. . . .

Neither do I think it shame to covenant with any knowing reader, that for a few years yet I may go on trust with him toward the payment of what I am now indebted, as being a work not to be raised from the heat of youth, or the vapours of wine, like that which flows at waste from the pen of some vulgar amorist, or the trencher fury of a rhyming parasite, not to be obtained by the invocation of Dame Memory and her Siren Daughters; but by devout prayer to that Eternal Spirit who can enrich with all utterance and knowledge, and sends out his Seraphim with the hallowed fire of his altar to touch and purify the lips of whom he pleases; to this must be added industrious and select reading, steady observation, insight into all seemly and generous arts and affairs; till which in some measure be compassed at mine own peril and cost, I refuse not to sustain this expectation from as many as are not loath to hazard so much credulity upon the best pledges that I can give them.

The Reason of Church Government Urg'd against Prelaty, 1642.

George Fox

THE magistrates were uneasy about me; but they could not agree what to do with me. One while they would have me sent up to the Parliament; another while they would have banished me to Ireland. At first they called me a deceiver, and a seducer, and a blasphemer; afterwards, when God had brought His plagues upon them, they said I was an honest, virtuous man. But their good report or bad report, their well speaking or ill speaking, was nothing to me; for the one did not lift me up, nor the other cast me down; praised be the Lord! At length they were made to turn me out of jail, about the beginning of winter, in the year 1651, after I had been a prisoner in Derby almost a year, six months in the house of correction, and the rest of the time in the common jail and dungeon.

Thus being set at liberty again, I went on, as before, in the work of the Lord; and as I was walking in a close with several Friends, I lifted up my head and espied three steeple-house spires, and they struck at my life. I asked them what place that was, and they said, Lichfield. Immediately the word of the Lord came to me that thither I must go. So, being come to the house we were going to, I bid Friends that were with me to walk into the house from me, saying nothing to them whither I was to go. As soon as they were gone I stepped away, and went by my eye over hedge and ditch till I came within a mile of Lichfield, where, in a great field, there were shepherds keeping their sheep. I was commanded by the Lord, of a sudden, to untie my shoes and put them off. I stood still, for it was winter, and the word of the Lord was like a fire in me, so I put off my shoes and was commanded to give them to the shepherds, and was to charge them to let no one have them except they paid for them. The poor shepherds trembled and were astonished.

Then I walked on about a mile till I came into the town, and as soon as I was got within the town the word of the Lord came to me again, to cry, "Woe unto the bloody city of Lichfield!" So I went up and down the streets, crying with a loud voice, "Woe to the bloody city of Lichfield!" It being market-day, I went into the market-place, and to and fro in the several parts of it, and made stands, crying as before, "Woe to the bloody city of Lichfield!" And no one laid hands on me; but as I went thus crying through the streets, there seemed to me to be a channel of blood running down the streets, and the market-place appeared like a pool of blood.

And so at last some Friends and friendly people came to me and said, "Alack, George, where are thy shoes?" I told them it was no matter.

Now when I had declared what was upon me, and cleared myself, I came out of the town in peace; and returning to the shepherds, gave them some money, and took my shoes of them again. But the fire of the Lord was so in my feet, that I did not matter to put on my shoes any more, and was at a stand whether I should or no, till I felt freedom from the Lord to do so; and as at last I came to a ditch and washed my feet, I put on my shoes again. After this a deep consideration came upon me, why, or for what reason, I should be sent to cry against that city, and call it the bloody city. For though the Parliament had the minster one while, and the King another, and much blood had been shed in the town during the wars between them, yet that could not be charged upon the town. But afterwards I came to understand that in the Emperor Dioclesian's time a thousand Christians were martyred in Lichfield, and so I must go in my stockings through the channel of their blood, and into the pool of their blood in the market-place, that I might raise up the memorial of the blood of those martyrs which had been shed above a thousand years before, and lay cold in their streets. So the sense of this blood was upon me, and I obeyed the word of the Lord. Ancient records testify how many of the Christian Britons suffered there. Much could I write of the sense I had of the blood of the martyrs that had been slain in this nation for the name of Christ, both under the ten persecutions and since; but I leave it to the Lord, and to His book, out of which all shall be judged; for His book is a most true record, and His Spirit a true recorder.

From his journal, 1651.

Thomas Ellwood

THE general quarter sessions for the peace coming on, my father, willing to excuse himself from a dirty journey, commanded me to get up betimes, and go to Oxford, and deliver in the recognizances he had taken; and bring him an account what justices were on the bench, and what principal pleas were before them; which he knew I knew how to do, having often attended him on those services.

I, who knew how it stood with me better than he did, felt a weight come over me as soon as he had spoken the word. For I presently saw it would bring a very great exercise upon me. But having never resisted his will in anything that was lawful, as this was, I attempted not to make any excuse, but, ordering a horse to be ready for me early in the morning, I went to bed, having great strugglings in my breast. For the enemy came upon me like a flood, and set many difficulties before me, swelling them up to the highest pitch, by representing them as mountains which I should never be able to get over; and alas! the faith which could remove mountains, and cast them into the sea, was but very small and weak in me. He cast into my mind not only how I should behave myself in court and dispatch the business I was sent about, but how I should demean myself towards my acquaintance, of which I had many in that city, with whom I was wont to be jolly; whereas now I could not put off my hat, nor bow to any of them, nor use the corrupt language of *you* to any one of them, but must keep to the plain and true language of *thou* and *thee*.

Much of this nature revolved in my mind, thrown in by the enemy to discourage and cast me down; and I had none to have recourse to for counsel or help, but to the Lord alone. To Him therefore I poured forth my supplications with earnest cries and breathings of soul, that He, in whom all power was, would enable me to go through this great exercise, and keep me faithful to Himself therein. And after some time He was pleased to compose my mind to stillness, and I went to rest.

Early next morning I got up, and found my spirit pretty calm and quiet, yet not without a fear upon me, lest I should slip and let fall the testimony which I had to bear. And as I rode, a frequent cry ran through me to the Lord, on this wise: "Oh my God, preserve me faithful, whatever befalls me! Suffer me not to be drawn into evil, how much scorn and contempt soever be cast upon me!"

Thus was my spirit exercised on the way almost continually. And when I was come within a mile or two of the city, whom should I meet upon the way coming from thence but Edward Burrough! I rode in a mountier cap (a dress more used then than now) and so did he; and because the weather was exceeding sharp, we both had drawn our caps down, to shelter our faces from the cold; and by that means neither of us knew the other, but passed by without taking notice one of the other; till a few days after, meeting again, and observing each other's dress, we recollected where we had so lately met. Then thought I within myself, Oh! how glad should I have been of a word of encouragement and counsel from him, when I was under that weighty exercise of mind! But the Lord saw it was not good for me, that my reliance might be wholly upon Him, and not on man.

When I had set up my horse, I went directly to the hall where the sessions were held, where I had been but a very little while before a knot of my old acquaintance espying me, came to me. One of them was a scholar in his gown, another a surgeon of that city, both my schoolfellows and fellow-boarders at Thame school, and the third a country gentleman, with whom I had long been very familiar.

When they were come up to me, they all saluted me after the usual manner, putting off their hats, and bowing, and saying "Your humble servant, sir;" expecting, no doubt, the like from me. But when they saw me stand still, not moving my cap, nor bowing my knee in any way of congee to them, they were amazed, and looked first one upon another, then upon me, and then one upon another again for a while, without a word speaking. At length the surgeon, a brisk young man, who stood nearest to me, clapping his hand in a familiar way upon my shoulder, and smiling on me, said: "What, Tom, a Quaker?" To which I readily and cheerfully answered, "Yes, a Quaker." And as the words passed out of my mouth, I felt joy spring in my heart, for I rejoiced that I had not been drawn out by them, into a compliance with them; and that I had strength and boldness given me, to confess myself to be one of that despised people.

The History of the Life of Thomas Ellwood,
written by himself, 1714.

W. B. Yeats

CERTAIN woods at Sligo, the woods above Dooney Rock and those above the waterfall at Ben Bulben, though I shall never perhaps walk there again, are so deep in my affections that I dream about them at night; and yet the woods at Coole, though they do not come into my dream, are so much more knitted to my thought that when I am dead they will have, I am persuaded, my longest visit. When we are dead, according to my belief, we live our lives backward for a certain number of years, treading the paths that we have trodden, growing young again, even childish again, till some attain an innocence that is no longer a mere accident of nature, but the human intellect's crowning achievement. It was at Coole that the first few simple thoughts that now, grown complex through their contact with other thoughts, explain the world, came to me from beyond my own mind. I practised meditations, and these, as I think, so affected my sleep that I began to have dreams that differed from ordinary dreams in seeming to take place amid brilliant light, and by their invariable coherence, and certain half-dreams, if I can call them so, between sleep and waking. I have noticed that such experiences come to me most often amid distraction, at some time that seems of all times the least fitting, as though it were necessary for the exterior mind to be engaged elsewhere, and it was during 1897 and 1898, when I was always just arriving from or just setting out to some political meeting, that the first dreams came. I was crossing a little stream near Inchy Wood and actually in the middle of a stride from bank to bank, when an emotion never experienced before swept down upon me. I said, "That is what the devout Christian feels, that is how he surrenders his will to the will of God." I felt an extreme surprise, for my whole imagination was preoccupied with the pagan mythology of ancient Ireland, I was marking in red ink, upon a large map, every sacred mountain. The next morning I awoke near dawn, to hear a voice saying, "The love of God is infinite for every human soul because every human soul is unique; no other can satisfy the same need in God."

Autobiographies, 1955.

Edwin Muir

WE left for Dresden about the end of March, and from the start loved the fine, spacious city. There during the hot, idle summer I seemed at last to recover from the long illness that had seized me when, at fourteen, I came to Glasgow. I realized that I must live over again the years which I had lived wrongly, and that every one should live his life twice, for the first attempt is always blind. I went over my life in that resting space, like a man who after travelling a long featureless road suddenly realises that, at this point or that, he had noticed almost without knowing it, with the corner of his eye, some extraordinary object, some rare treasure, yet in his sleep-walking had gone on, consciously aware only of the blank road flowing back beneath his feet. These objects, like Griseldas, were all patiently waiting at the points where I had first ignored them, and my full gaze could take in things which an absent glance had once passed over unseeingly, so that life I had wasted was returned to me.

> And with ane blenk it come into his thocht,
> That he sumtime hir face bifore had sene.

In living that life over again I struck up a first acquaintance with myself. Till now, I realised that I had been stubbornly staring away from myself. As if I had no more choice than time, I had walked with my face immovably set forward, as incapable as time of turning my head and seeing what was behind me. I looked, and what I saw was myself as I had lived up to that moment when I could turn my head. I had been existing, to use Holms's phrase, merely as something which consisted of "the words with which one tries to explain it"; so that when at last I looked back at that life which, whatever I might think of it, was the life I knew best, it seemed to me that I was not seeing my own life merely, but all human life, and I became conscious of it as a strange and unique process. In turning my head and looking *against* the direction in which time was hurrying me, I won a new kind of experience; for now that I no longer marched in step with time I could see life timelessly and with that in terms of the imagination. I felt, though I had not the ability to express it, what Proust describes in *Le Temps Retrouvé*. "A moment liberated from the order of time" seemed actually to have re-created in me "a man to feel it who was also freed from the order of time". But as this kind of looking required the use of the imagination, it wakened my imagination, sluggishly at first. I did not feel so much that I was rediscovering the world of life as that I was discovering it for the first time.

I was thirty-five then, and passing through a stage which, if things had been different, I should have reached ten years earlier. I have felt that handicap ever since. I began to write poetry at thirty-five instead of at twenty-five or twenty.

An Autobiography, 1954.

John Keats

MY DEAR HESSEY—You are very good in sending me the letters from the *Chronicle*—and I am very bad in not acknowledging such a kindness sooner—pray forgive me. It so chanced that I have had that paper every day—I have seen today's. I cannot but feel indebted to those gentlemen who have taken my part. As for the rest, I begin to get a little acquainted with my own strength and weakness. Praise or blame has but a momentary effect on the man whose love of beauty in the abstract makes him a severe critic on his own works. My own domestic criticism has given me pain without comparison beyond what Blackwood or the *Quarterly* could possibly inflict—and also when I feel I am right, no external praise can give me such a glow as my own solitary reperception and ratification of what is fine. J. S. is perfectly right in regard to the slipshod *Endymion*. That it is so is no fault of mine. No! though it may sound a little paradoxical. It is as good as I had power to make it—by myself. Had I been nervous about its being a perfect piece, and with that view asked advice, and trembled over every page, it would not have been written; for it is not in my nature to fumble. I will write independently. I have written independently without judgment. I may write independently, and with judgment, hereafter. The Genius of Poetry must work out its own salvation in a man: it cannot be matured by law and precept, but by sensation and watchfulness in itself. That which is creative must create itself. In *Endymion*, I leaped headlong into the sea, and thereby have become better acquainted with the soundings, the quicksands and the rocks, than if I had stayed upon the green shore and piped a silly pipe, and took tea and comfortable advice. I was never afraid of failure; for I would sooner fail than not be among the greatest. But I am nigh getting into a rant.

A letter to J. A. Hessey, October 9th, 1818.

Richard Jefferies

I WAS not more than eighteen when an inner and esoteric meaning began to come to me from all the visible universe, and indefinable aspirations filled me. I found them in the grass fields, under the trees, on the hill-tops at sunrise, and in the night. There was a deeper meaning everywhere. The sun burned with it, the broad front of morning beamed with it; a deep feeling entered me while gazing at the sky in the azure noon, and in the star-lit evening.

I was sensitive to all things, to the earth under, and the star-hollow round about; to the last blade of grass, to the largest oak. They seemed like exterior nerves and veins for the conveyance of feeling to me. Sometimes a very ecstasy of exquisite enjoyment of the entire visible universe filled me. I was aware that in reality the feeling and the thought were in me, and not in the earth or sun; yet I was more conscious of it when in company with these. I began to make efforts to express these thoughts in writing, but could not succeed to my own liking. Time went on, and harder experiences, and the pressure of labour came, but in no degree abated the fire of first thought. Again and again I made resolutions that I would write it, in some way or other, and as often failed. I could express any other idea with ease, but not this. Once especially I remember, in a short interval of distasteful labour, walking away to a spot by a brook which skirts an ancient Roman wall, and there trying to determine and really commence to work. Again I failed. More time, more changes, and still the same thought running beneath everything.

At last, in 1880, in the old castle of Pevensey, under happy circumstances, once more I resolved, and actually did write down a few notes. Even then I could not go on, but I kept the notes (I had destroyed all former beginnings), and in the end, two years afterwards, commenced this book.

The Story of my Heart, 1883.

Eric Gill

THE thing to be told at this place is that by reason of an apparently irrelevant happening I broke through the inhibition and started a stone carving of a young woman. The irrelevant happening was the comparative continence caused by the approaching birth of our youngest daughter. In the absurd refinement of our puritanical civilisation these things aren't talked about, so I have very little idea as to what goes on in the minds or bodies of my fellow-men, and practically nothing at all as to what goes on in the minds of those whom I may call my fellow-women, but this book, though necessarily more or less absurd, need not be refined. So I am at liberty to say that as I couldn't have all I wanted in one way I determined to see what I could do about it in another—I fashioned a woman of *stone*. Up to that time, I had never made what is called an "erotic" drawing of any sort, and least of all in so laborious a medium as stone. And so, just as on the first occasion when, with immense planning and scheming, I touched my lover's lovely body, I insisted on seeing her completely naked (no peeping between the uncut pages, so to say), so my first erotic drawing was not on the back of an envelope but a week or so's work on a decent piece of hard stone. I say this seems praiseworthy, and so it is. But I give God the praise and am as duly thankful as a self-conscious human being can be. I don't think it was a very good carving, and in spite of all I have said, no one would guess the fervours which conditioned its making. But there it was; it was a carving of a naked young woman, and if I hadn't very much wanted a naked young woman, I don't think I should ever have done it. Lord, how exciting!—and not merely touching and seeing but actually making her. I was responsible for her very existence and her every form came straight from my heart. A new world opened before me. My Lord! can't you see it? Letter-cutting—a grand job, and as grand as ever—the grandest job in the world. What could be better? If you've never cut letters in a good piece of stone, with hammer and chisel, you can't know. And this new job was the same job, only the letters were different ones. A new alphabet—the word was made flesh.

Autobiography, 1940.

B. R. Haydon

I was going on with another work, and I had not had a shilling for weeks but what I had borrowed, or got from selling book after book, my clothes, everything. I deliberated, not that I ever hesitated, but because I was determined to take a clear view of my position. Naturally my heart and mind turned to Wilkie, and I thought it strange that I had never heard a word, or received a call from him, nor in fact heard from any friend his feelings on the subject of my position.

I resolved, therefore, to call on him, and hear what he would say; for as his advice was always cautious, I imagined it was the best thing I could do.

First, however, I went to a friend, and said, "What is to be done?" "That I can't tell you," said he, with a cold, withdrawing air. I left him in pain, and walked quietly to Wilkie. I told him I wanted the common necessities of life. He looked at me with horror. I said, "Will you advance me £10 in addition to the £24 I owe you?" He shook, got nervous, was oppressed by my presence, looked cold, heartless, distant, and fearful I would stay long. He stammered out he could not spare more. I urged on him that he risked all by not helping me now. He persisted he could not. He kept saying, "I told you so, I told you so." He was frightened out of his life. This was such a palpable blow at me as a mark of disapprobation for my daring to attack the Academy and refute Payne Knight, that he feared almost to acknowledge he had ever known me at all.

I walked out without saying a word, and Wilkie seemed delighted at being relieved of my presence. He considered me a ruined man, and thought the sooner he disengaged himself the better.

Ah, Wilkie, the pang I suffered at that moment was more on your account than on my own!

Never shall I forget my melancholy walk through Kensington Gardens back to London.

What should I do? I owed my landlord £200. How was I to go on? Would he allow it? How was I to dine—to live, in fact? A large picture just rubbed in—in want that day of a dinner. Shall I give up my "Solomon", relinquish my schemes, sell all, retire to obscure lodgings, and do anything for a living? It would be praiseworthy—it would be more. But if I did, I never could realise enough to pay my debts. Surely it would be wiser to make another cast—to dismiss despair. I was in health; I had no family. I knew myself capable of submitting to anything, but once such a situation is relinquished, it is not possible to regain it again. Besides, the apparent cowardice, after preaching such heroic doctrines to the students! The apparent cowardice was nothing if I could approach nearer my grand object by it, but I thought I could not by submission do so—and then the meanness! How could I submit, who had told the students that failure should stimulate and not depress? Contemptible! How bear my own reflections—how the reflections of others, knowing I deserved them? Something instantly circulated through me like an essence

of fire, and striding with wider steps, I determined to bear all—
not to yield one particle of my designs—to go at once for my
model—to begin tomorrow, and to make the most of my actual
situation. "Well done," said the god within, and instantly I was
invincible. I went to the house where I had always dined, intend-
ing to dine without paying for that day. I thought the servants
did not offer me the same attention. I thought I perceived the
company examine me—I thought the meat was worse. My
heart sank as I said falteringly, "I will pay you tomorrow."
The girl smiled and seemed interested. As I was escaping with a
sort of lurking horror, she said, "Mr Haydon, Mr Haydon, my
master wishes to see you." "My God," thought I, "it is to tell
me he can't trust!" In I walked like a culprit. "Sir, I beg your
pardon, but I see by the papers you have been ill-used; I hope
you won't be angry—I mean no offence; but—you won't be
offended—I just wish to say, as you have dined here many years
and always paid, if it would be a convenience during your present
work to dine here till it is done—you know—so that you may not
be obliged to spend your money here, when you may want it—
I was going to say you need be under no apprehension—hem!
for a dinner."

My heart really filled. I told him I would take his offer. The
good man's forehead was perspiring, and he seemed quite
relieved. From that hour the servants (who were pretty girls)
eyed me with a lustrous regret, and redoubled their attentions.
The honest wife said, if I was ever ill she would send me broth
or any such little luxury, and the children used to cling round
my knees and ask me to draw a face. "Now," said I, as I walked
home with an elastic step, "now for my landlord." I called up
Perkins, and laid my desperate case before him. He was quite
affected. I said, "Perkins, I'll leave you if you wish it, but it will
be a pity, will it not, not to finish such a beginning?" Perkins
looked at the rubbing in, and muttered, "It's a grand thing—
how long will it be before it is done, Sir?" "Two years." "What,
two years more, and no rent?" "Not a shilling." He rubbed his
chin, and muttered, "I should not like ye to go—it's hard for both

of us; but what I say is this, you always paid me when you could, and why should you not again when you are able?" "That's what I say." "Well, sir, here is my hand" (and a great fat one it was). "I'll give you two years more, and if this does not sell" (affecting to look very severe) "why then, Sir, we'll consider what is to be done; so don't fret, but work."

Having thus relieved my mind of its two heavy loads, I knelt down and prayed with all my soul, and rose up refreshed and buoyant.

The Life of Benjamin Robert Haydon, historical painter,
from his *Autobiography and Journals,* 1853.

Joseph Conrad

I WILL make bold to say that neither at sea nor ashore have I ever lost the sense of responsibility. There is more than one sort of intoxication. Even before the most seductive reveries I have remained mindful of that sobriety of the interior life, that asceticism of sentiment, in which alone the naked form of truth, such as one conceives it, can be rendered without shame. It is but a maudlin and indecent verity that comes out through the strength of wine. I have tried to be a sober worker all my life—all my two lives. I did so from taste, no doubt, having an instinctive horror of losing my sense of full self-possession, but also from artistic conviction. Yet there are so many pitfalls on each side of the path that, having gone some way, and feeling a little battered and weary, as a middle-aged traveller will from the mere daily difficulties of the march, I ask myself whether I have kept always, always faithful to that sobriety wherein there is power, and truth, and peace.

A Personal Record, 1919.

Biographical Index

ARCH, Joseph, 1826–1919 (p. 60). Himself a farm-labourer, he was one of the pioneer organisers of agricultural workers' unions, and was eventually returned to Parliament. His narrated life-story was edited with a preface by the Countess of Warwick, and appeared in 1898.

AUBREY, John, 1626–1697 (p. 64). Antiquary and early member of the Royal Society. Among the *Brief Lives*, which he wrote after he began to collaborate with Anthony Wood on *Athenae Oxoniensis*, is an autobiographical fragment, from which these paragraphs are taken. Andrew Clark's two-volume edition of *Brief Lives* appeared in 1898, and an edition by Anthony Powell was brought out by the Cresset Press, 1939.

BARBELLION, W. N. P., 1889–1919 (p. 182). His real name was Bruce Frederick Cummings. He held a post in the Natural History Museum, and waged a long and courageous battle against mortal illness. *The Journal of a Disappointed Man*, extracts from notebooks kept over many years, was published by Chatto & Windus just before his death. His *Last Diary*, in the following year, had an introduction by his brother which revealed his identity.

BAXTER, Richard, 1615–1691 (p. 90). An eminent Puritan divine, author of many religious and polemical works. After his death, a mass of autobiographical and historical material, known as *Reliquiae Baxterianae*, was edited by his friend Matthew Sylvester and published in 1695. Edmund Calamy made an *Abridgement* of the autobiographical documents, which was published in 1702, but the first shortened version of Baxter's Life in his own words is *The Autobiography of Richard Baxter*, edited by J. M. Lloyd Thomas, published in 1925 and now available in the Everyman Library.

BELLAMY, George Anne, ?1731–1788 (p. 137). An actress, who played Juliet to Garrick's Romeo while she was still in her teens, and who at the height of her fame made plenty of money; but after a stormy life she died bankrupt, somewhat soured by misfortune but not self-pitying. Her lively memoirs were published in six volumes in Dublin in 1785.

BLAKE, William, 1757–1827 (p. 195). Poet, painter and engraver. This passage comes from a letter to his friend and patron Thomas Butts, written when he was nearing the end of his stay at Felpham under the aegis of the well-intentioned but obtuse William Hayley.

BOSWELL, James, 1740–1795 (p. 157). Johnson's biographer, who wrote about himself with almost unexampled zeal. His London Journal was written partly for the benefit of his friend John Johnson. This and the later private journals have been discovered and made available only in recent years, and not all the Boswell papers are yet published. *The London Journal 1760–1763* was first issued in 1950, with an introduction and notes by Frederick A. Pottle, Yale University Press. It is available as an Ace paperback.

BROWNE, Thomas, 1605–1682 (p. 77). Physician and antiquary, knighted by Charles II. *Religio Medici*, composed when he was about thirty, was printed surreptitiously in 1642; an authorised edition appeared in the following year. The best text is that edited by J. J. Denonain, Cambridge University Press, 1953.

BROWNING, Elizabeth Barrett, 1806–1861 (p. 109). A poet in her own right, she married Robert Browning in 1846, after leading the life of an invalid for years, and was restored to health and happiness. There are several collections of Mrs Browning's letters. This extract, from a long explanatory letter written soon after her wedding, comes from an edition by F. G. Kenyon, 1897.

BUNYAN, John, 1628–1688 (p. 187). Baptist preacher and author of *The Pilgrim's Progress*, whose spiritual auto-biography, *Grace Abounding to the Chief of Sinners*, was published in 1666, after a period of imprisonment for un-licensed preaching. This passage comes from *A Relation of the Imprisonment of John Bunyan*, which, though it recounts events that took place in 1660, was not published till 1765. It can now be read in the Everyman edition of *Grace Abounding*.

BURNEY, Fanny, 1752–1840 (p. 138). Novelist and diarist. Her *Evelina*, published anonymously in 1778, won her the admiration of Dr Johnson, who became a devoted friend. She held a position at Court, and married General D'Arblay, a French refugee, in 1793. Her *Diary and Letters* were edited by her niece, seven volumes appearing between 1842 and 1846. There have been several more recent selections.

BURNS, Robert, 1759–1796 (p. 142). The poet wrote a long autobiographical letter to Dr John Moore in 1797, and kept a journal; his verse is full of personal detail. Robert Chambers compiled the *Life and Works of Robert Burns*, interspersing biographical material with the poems, so that each might illuminate the other. A revised and enlarged edition in four volumes, edited by William Wallace, was published at Edinburgh in 1896.

BURTON, Isabel (Lady), 1831–1896 (p. 113). Born Arundell, she married Richard Burton, the explorer and translator of

The Book of the Thousand and one Nights, in 1861, after a
long and star-crossed courtship. She first encountered Burton
when she was nineteen. The text is from *The Romance of
Isabel Lady Burton, the Story of her Life,* told in part by
herself and in part by W. H. Wilkins, 1897.

BYRON, George Gordon Noel, Lord, 1786–1824 (p. 81). The
poet's memoirs were destroyed after his death by his publisher,
at the urgent request of his wife and literary executors; but
from his letters and journals we gather an extremely lively
impression of his complex and fascinating personality. An
edition of his *Letters and Journals* by Thomas Moore appeared
in 1830; the standard edition, in 6 volumes, is by R. E.
Prothero, 1898–1901. *Byron: a Self-portrait,* compiled by
Peter Quennell from letters, diaries, etc, came out in 1950.

CARLYLE, Jane, 1801–1866 (p. 170). Born Welsh, she married
Thomas Carlyle in 1826. They moved in 1828 to Craigenputtock, where he wrote *Sartor Resartus.* A selection of Mrs
Carlyle's admirable letters, edited by Trudy Bliss, was
published by Gollancz in 1950 and is available in the Gray
Arrow series. The letter from which this extract is taken was
written to Miss Mary Smith, a school-teacher in Carlisle, and
appeared in her *Autobiography,* 1892.

CARLYLE, Thomas, 1795–1881 (p. 172). The historian and
Sage of Chelsea committed to paper, soon after the death of his
wife in 1866, some recollections of their married life. These
were not intended for publication, but were printed by J. A.
Froude in 1881 in a volume of Carlyle papers entitled
Reminiscences.

CAVENDISH, Margaret, Duchess of Newcastle, ?1624–
1674 (p. 126). Born Lucas, she married as his second wife
William, Duke of Newcastle, whose biography she wrote.
She also wrote many plays, poems and essays, and was a

notable eccentric. Her autobiography was first published at the private press of Lee Priory in 1814, edited with an introduction by Sir Egerton Brydges.

CHARKE, Charlotte, ?–1760 (p. 57). A daughter of the actor-playwright Colley Cibber. There are no dates in her extremely amusing autobiography, which probably contains a fair amount of fiction. This extract comes from a section entitled "An account of her birth, education and mad pranks committed in her youth." The book itself appeared in instalments in 1755. It was included in Hunt and Clark's collection, *Autobiography*, published 1826–1834, and in *Constable's Miscellany* in 1929.

CHESTERTON, G. K., 1874–1936 (p. 99). Essayist, poet and journalist. His *Autobiography* was published by Hutchinson in 1936.

CIBBER, Colley, 1671–1767 (p. 141). An actor and dramatist who, oddly enough, was made Poet Laureate in 1730. He became the hero of *The Dunciad* in the 1742 edition of the poem, having had some unfortunate brushes with Pope.

CLARE, John, 1793–1864 (p. 50). The son of a Northampton-shire labourer, his first volume of poems was published in 1820 and brought him a London as well as a local reputation. Four volumes were published before he became insane in 1837. His autobiographical sketches were first published in 1927 by Cobden-Sanderson, with an introduction, notes and additions by Edmund Blunden.

COBBETT, William, 1763–1835 (p. 49). Pamphleteer, journalist and commentator on the social and economic scene, a man of immense energy. His works contain much autobiographical material, which has been assembled into a continuous narrative by William Reitzel. This was published by

Faber in 1933 as *The Progress of a Ploughboy*, and re-issued in 1947 with the title *The Autobiography of William Cobbett*.

COLERIDGE, S. T., 1772–1834 (p. 24). The *Biographia Literaria*, 1817, is of course an autobiographical work, in which the poet and critic reveals much about his intellectual development; but his letters reveal more about his day-to-day existence. In 1797 he wrote a series of letters to his friend Thomas Poole of Nether Stowey, recording something of his life before he went up to Cambridge. His *Correspondence* was first edited by E. H. Coleridge, 1895.

COLLINGWOOD, R. G., 1889–1943 (p. 72). His *Autobiography* was written while he was Waynflete Professor of Metaphysical Philosophy at Oxford.

CONRAD, Joseph, 1857–1924 (p. 213). Novelist. Of Polish origin; Korzeniowski was his name before he took British nationality. He turned to the writing of novels after a career in the merchant navy.

COWLEY, Abraham, 1618–1667 (p. 77). Poet and essayist. A sumptuous edition of his *Essays* was published posthumously in 1688, with a preface by Thomas Sprat of Royal Society fame. A volume of Cowley's poetry and prose, edited by L. C. Martin, was published by the Oxford University Press in 1949.

COWPER, William, 1731–1800 (p. 167). Poet and letter-writer. The *Memoir* from which this extract comes was probably written in 1765, soon after his recovery from a complete mental breakdown. It contains a quiet and dreadful account of his temptations to suicide, and his actual attempts to end his life by various means. It would probably not have been written except for his Evangelical conversion, and it was not published until sixteen years after his death.

DARWIN, Charles, 1809–1882 (p. 92). The great naturalist's autobiography, concluded in 1876, first appeared as part of the *Life and Letters*, edited by his son Francis, 1887. His grand-daughter Nora Barlow has edited a revised edition, in which passages previously omitted are restored. This was published by Collins, 1958.

DAVIES, W. H., 1871–1940 (p. 154). Poet and vagabond, whose *Autobiography of a Super-Tramp* appeared in 1908 with a preface by Bernard Shaw.

DUNTON, John, 1659–1733 (p. 146). Publisher and book-seller, and writer of political pamphlets. The eccentricity of his autobiography and of his own character is well indicated by the original title page.

ELLWOOD, Thomas, 1639–1713 (p. 201). An eminent member of the Society of Friends. The episode recounted took place in 1659, soon after his conversion to Quakerism through the preaching of Edward Burrough.

FANSHAWE, Anne, 1625–1679 (p. 124). Born Harrison, she married Sir Richard Fanshawe, who later became Charles II's Ambassador to the Courts of Portugal and Spain. Her *Memoirs*, written in 1676 for her "most dear and only" surviving son, were edited by Beatrice Marshall and first published in 1905. Their prime purpose was to tell her orphaned son about his distinguished father; but they also give a most attractive picture of the writer, whose spirit stood up to all manner of adventures and misfortunes.

FOX, George, 1624–1691 (p. 199). The founder of the Society of Friends. His Journal proper closes in June 1675, but he dictated his life-story from notebooks and papers to his son-in-law Thomas Lower. Thomas Ellwood and others collected material relating to the last sixteen years of his life, made a continuous narrative of it and cast it in autobiographical terms. This Ellwood text of the Journals was first published in 1694. The handiest edition is that in the Everyman's Library. The episode recounted here took place in 1651.

FRY, Elizabeth, 1780–1845 (p. 83). The Quaker philanthropist and preacher, best known for her work among the women prisoners at Newgate. One of the Gurneys of Earlham, she married Joseph Fry in 1820 and had a large family. Her life-story was compiled from her journals by two of her daughters, and issued in 1847 as *Memoir of Elizabeth Fry.*

FYNES-CLINTON, Henry, 1781–1852 (p. 175). A distin-guished classical scholar. His *Literary Remains* were edited by his brother in 1854. This passage comes from his brief autobiography contained therein, and refers to the loss of his first wife. She died after seven months of marriage, having given birth to a premature child, who did not survive.

GIBBON, Edward, 1737–1794 (p. 82). The great historian of the Roman Empire left several autobiographical documents, which were worked into a continuous narrative and published as *The Autobiography of Edward Gibbon* by his friend the Earl of Sheffield in 1796. This passage, however, comes from his third Journal. *Gibbon's Journal* was edited with intro-ductory notes by D. M. Low, Chatto & Windus, 1929.

GILL, Eric, 1882–1940 (p. 209). Stone-carver, engraver, typo-grapher and writer on religious-philosophical-political themes.

GOSSE, Edmund (Sir), 1849–1928 (p. 35). Literary historian and man of letters. His *Father and Son,* a remarkable study of his upbringing in a rigidly pious home, was published anonymously in 1907, by Heinemann.

GRAY, Thomas, 1716–1771 (p. 85). The *Correspondence*

of the poet, who was an admirable letter-writer, was edited by Paget Toynbee and Leonard Whibley, Oxford University Press, 1935. This letter was written towards the end of the Grand Tour which Gray made with Horace Walpole.

GREENE, Robert, ?1560–1592 (p. 79). Writer of plays, pamphlets and romances. His *Groatsworth of Wit bought with a Million of Repentence* is famous for its attack on Shakespeare. This extract comes from another penitential pamphlet, *The Repentance of Robert Greene Master of Arts*, published in 1592, the same year as the *Groatsworth*. These autobiographical pieces have been reprinted in a single volume in the Bodley Head Quartos, edited by G. B. Harrison, 1923.

HALKETT, Anne, 1622–1699 (p. 112). Born Murray, she married Sir James Halkett in 1656, after a long love-affair with Joseph Bamfield, a Royalist colonel who enlisted her aid in his plot to smuggle the Duke of York out of England in 1648. Her autobiography, written about 1678, was published for the Camden Society in 1875, edited by J. G. Nichols and S. R. Gardiner.

HARE, Augustus, 1834–1903 (p. 33). Best known for his Guide Books, but also the author of the most massive autobiography in the English language. The first three volumes of *The Story of my Life* were published in 1896, the next three in 1900, and Hare continued to work at his journal till his death. The vast memoirs have been reduced to two entertaining volumes by Malcolm Barnes, *The Years with Mother*, 1952, and *The Solitary Years*, 1953, Allen & Unwin.

HAYDON, B. R., 1786–1846 (p. 210). A grandiose painter, who impressed himself on his contemporaries, but who is known to posterity mainly on account of his delightful autobiography. Lasting success eluded him, and he took his own life. Tom Taylor's edition was reprinted with an introduction by Aldous Huxley in 1926, and in 1927 G. Bell & Son published *Autobiography and Memoirs of Benjamin Robert Haydon*, compiled from the *Autobiography and Journals* and *Correspondence and Table Talk* by A. D. P. Penrose.

HAZLITT, William, 1788–1830 (p. 183). Essayist and critic, and a gifted painter. This passage comes from an essay written in 1828, provoked by Leigh Hunt's remarks in *Lord Byron and his Contemporaries*.

HERBERT, Edward, Lord Herbert of Cherbury, 1583–1648 (p. 149). Philosopher, poet, diplomatist. His entertaining autobiography was written about 1643, but not published until 1764, when Horace Walpole printed it at his Strawberry Hill press. It was edited with an introduction, notes, appendices and a continuation of the life, by Sir Sidney Lee, 1886, second (revised) edition 1906.

HERBERT, George, 1593–1633 (p. 189). Priest and poet, younger brother of Lord Herbert of Cherbury. On his deathbed he entrusted his poems to his friend Nicholas Ferrar's care, and it was he who brought out *The Temple* in 1633. In the poem *Affliction* Herbert refers to his life at Cambridge and his long-deferred decision to take holy orders.

HICKEY, William, 1749–1830 (p. 131). He had a chequered career as an attorney, and travelled extensively, especially in India. His long and amusing memoirs were first published 1913–1925, by Hurst & Blackett, edited by Alfred Spence. An unbowdlerised but abridged version, edited by Peter Quennell, was published by Hutchinson, 1960.

HOLCROFT, Thomas, 1745–1809 (p. 20). Playwright, actor, journalist and active Radical. His excellent autobiography covers only the first fifteen years of his life, which included a spell at Newmarket as a stable-boy. His *Memoirs* were completed by Hazlitt and published in 1816. A new edition of the memoirs, edited by Elbridge Colby, was published in 1925 by Constable.

HUDSON, W. H., 1841–1922 (p. 16). Naturalist, essayist and writer of romances. Born near Buenos Aires of American parents, he became a British subject in 1900.

HUME, David, 1711–1776 (p. 101). Philosopher, political economist and historian. He left an autobiography which was published after his death by his friend Adam Smith, but this extract comes from *A Treatise of Human Nature*, 1739.

HUTCHINSON, Lucy, 1620–1671 (p. 26). Born Apsley, she married in 1638 John Hutchinson, governor of Nottingham during the Civil War, who eventually became a regicide and a member of Cromwell's first two Councils of State. She wrote her famous *Memoirs of the Life of Colonel Hutchinson* between 1664–1671, and also wrote a fragmentary autobiography. These were first published in 1810.

JEFFERIES, Richard, 1848–1887 (p. 208). Essayist and naturalist. He meditated *The Story of my Heart*, a sort of spiritual autobiography, for some seventeen years before it was first published in 1883.

JOHNSON, Samuel, 1709–1784 (p. 22). Critic, poet and lexicographer. Boswell records that shortly before his death, Johnson "in a most precipitate manner" burned masses of his papers. The account of his early life, from which this passage is taken, was rescued in a fragmentary state by his negro servant Francis Barber, whose widow sold it to the proprietor of the museum at Lichfield. It was published in 1805.

JOYCE, Matthias, 1754–1786 (p. 176). One of the early Methodist ministers, whose autobiographies were collected by T. Jackson in his *Lives of the Early Methodist Preachers*,

1837. An Irishman, born in Dublin of a Roman Catholic father and a Protestant mother, Joyce spent a wild and rebellious boyhood, which was followed by conversion and a devoted ministry.

KEATS, John, 1795–1821 (p. 207). The poet left no auto-biography, but from his letters we get a remarkably vivid impression of his personality. This passage comes from a letter written just after the unfavourable reviews of *Endymion*. The *Letters* have been edited by M. Buxton Forman, and there is also an edition by Sidney Colvin.

KEMBLE, Fanny, 1809–1893 (p. 139). The daughter of Charles and Maria Theresa Kemble, both stars of the theatre, she made her first stage appearance as Juliet in 1829 at a Covent Garden production of *Romeo and Juliet*, in which her father played Mercutio. She made an unhappy marriage, lived for years in the United States, and produced a long series of very lively reminiscences.

KEMPE, Margery, ?1373–? (p. 184). A citizen's wife of Lynn, mother of many children, and a religious visionary; she dictated her life-story, which deals with both mundane and spiritual affairs, referring to herself as "this creature". Hers is the earliest extant autobiography in English. The only known MS dates from the middle of the fifteenth century. A modern-ised version by W. Butler Bowden is available in the World's Classics.

LACKINGTON, James, 1746–1816 (p. 56). Bookseller. An entirely self-made man, shrewd and cocksure, his bookshop in Finsbury Square was known as "The Temple of the Muses."

LAMB, Charles, 1775–1834 (p. 132). Essayist, who often wrote about his own experiences, sometimes under the guise of

Elia. When Lamb was staying with Coleridge at Nether Stowey in 1797, he met William and Dorothy Wordsworth. Lamb's *Letters* were edited by Talfourd in 1837, but the definitive edition is by E. V. Lucas, 1935.

LEAR, Edward, 1812–1888 (p. 148). Artist, traveller and author of nonsense verses. His *Book of Nonsense* (illustrated limericks) appeared in 1846, the *Nonsense Songs, Stories and Botany* in 1870.

LEIGH HUNT, James, 1784–1859 (p. 52). Journalist, essayist, editor of *The Examiner*. In 1828 he published *Lord Byron and his Contemporaries, with recollections of the Author's Life and of his Visit to Italy*. Much of this material reappears in *The Autobiography*, 1850, which was revised and slightly shortened in 1859. Shelley takes Byron's place as the main hero.

MARTINDALE, Adam, 1623–1686 (p. 145). A non-conformist minister and schoolmaster, of Lancashire yeoman stock, who wrote his own Life about 1685. It was published in the annals of the Chetham Society in 1843, edited from the MS in the British Museum by the Rev. Richard Parkinson.

MARTINEAU, Harriet, 1802–1876 (p. 116). Voluminous writer on social reform and on religious and philosophical topics; translator, historian and novelist. Her autobiography contains an extremely vivid account of her unhappy and repressed childhood, besides interesting comments on the great literary figures of her day.

MILL, J. S., 1806–1873 (p. 165). Philosopher and writer on political reform. He was subjected to a most rigorous and intensive education by his father, James Mill, the utilitarian philosopher. After the breakdown described in this passage of his autobiography, J. S. Mill based his life and thinking on more broadly humanist principles.

MILTON, John, 1608–1674 (p. 197). Poet and pamphleteer. Several of his politico-religious treatises contain interesting autobiographical passages.

MOORE, George, 1852–1933 (p. 134). Novelist, who wrote several volumes of distinguished autobiographical gossip.

MUIR, Edwin, 1882–1959 (p. 205). Poet and critic. An account of his life appeared in 1940 as *The Story and the Fable*, and a revised and enlarged version, *An Autobiography*, in 1954.

NEWMAN, J. H., Cardinal, 1801–1890 (p. 191). His *Apologia pro Vita Sua* appeared in 1864, nineteen years after he had been received into the Roman Catholic Church, in answer to Charles Kingsley's misrepresentations in *Macmillan's Magazine*. It appeared serially, and in 1865 was published, with the omission of much controversial matter and a few modifications, as *History of my Religious Opinions*.

NORTH, Roger, The Hon., 1654–1734 (p. 53). Barrister and landowner, the fifth son of Dudley, 4th Lord North. He wrote about his distinguished brothers in *The Lives of the Norths*, which was published in 1740. His own autobiography concludes with the death of his brother Francis, Lord Keeper Guilford, in 1685. It was edited in 1887 by Augustus Jessop, with an informative introduction.

NUGENT, Maria (Lady), 1771–1834 (p. 119). The daughter of an American loyalist, Cortlandt Skinner, she was born in New Jersey but brought up in England, where her family moved after the Revolution. In 1797 she married George Nugent, who in 1801 became Lieutenant-Governor of Jamaica. He later received a baronetcy and served as Commander-in-Chief in India. This extract comes from *Lady Nugent's Journal, Jamaica a Hundred Years Ago*, reprinted from a journal kept from 1801 to 1815, and issued for private circulation in 1839. It was edited by F. Cundall and published by A. & C. Black in 1907.

OSBALDESTON, George, 1787–1866 (p. 151). The most famous sportsman of his day; a Yorkshire landowner with a passion for betting, who owned and rode racehorses, was a M.F.H., a crack shot and a cricketer. His *Autobiography*, edited by E. D. Cuming and Sir T. A. Cook, was published in 1926.

OSBORNE, Dorothy, 1627–1695 (p. 121). Married Sir William Temple in 1655, after much opposition from her father and brothers. Her delightful letters to Temple, covering the years 1652–1654 were first published in 1888, and were edited by G. Moore Smith for the Oxford University Press in 1928.

OWEN, R. D., 1801–1877 (p. 38). The son of Robert Owen the social philanthropist and reformer. He spent much of his life in America, and his autobiographical sketches, covering the first twenty-seven years of his life, were contributed to *The Atlantic Monthly*, and were published in London in 1874. The episode referred to here took place when Robert Dale Owen was about eleven years old.

PATTISON, Mark, 1813–1884 (p. 66). He eventually became Rector of Lincoln College, Oxford, after an intrigue (bitterly resented) had robbed him of the rectorship in 1851. The *Memoirs*, dictated in 1883 and published in 1885, give an interesting picture of Tractarian Oxford and of Pattison's very prickly personality.

PAWSON, John, 1737–1806 (p. 135). Methodist minister, more esteemed for his pastoral work than for his preaching, who made a very edifying end. His autobiography is included in Vol. II of T. Jackson's *Lives of Early Methodist Preachers*, 1837.

BIOGRAPHICAL INDEX

PEPYS, Samuel, 1633–1703 (p. 160). Secretary to the Admiralty. His *Diary* covers the period January 1660 to May 1669, when he abandoned it because of his failing eyesight. It was deciphered by John Smith and first edited by Lord Braybrooke in 1825. More nearly complete editions and many selections have since been published.

PRIOR, Matthew, 1664–1721 (p. 153). Diplomatist and accomplished writer of light verse. A sumptuous edition of his *Poems* came out in 1718, and his *Writings* were edited by A. R. Waller for the Cambridge University Press, 1905–1907.

DE QUINCEY, Thomas, 1785–1859 p. 177). Essayist. His autobiographical *Confessions of an English Opium Eater* first appeared in 1822, a new and enlarged edition in 1856. It is available in the World's Classics.

ROBINSON, Mary, 1758–1800 (p. 29). The beautiful actress known as Perdita, who was painted by Reynolds, Gainsborough, Romney, Hoppner and others. Her memoirs break off with her estrangement from the Prince Regent in 1791. They were written in 1800 and finished by her daughter, who had them published in 1801. Mrs Robinson wrote novels and poems after she gave up the stage, and her *Memoirs* have something of the quality of a novel, mirroring "an ingenuous, affectionate, susceptible heart".

RUSKIN, John, 1819–1900 (p. 30). Art critic and writer on social reform. *Praeterita*, a review of some of the places, books and people that influenced his development, is the only one of his works intended solely to give pleasure. It was published in 28 paper-bound parts between 1885 and 1889. An edition with an introduction by Sir Kenneth Clark was published by Rupert Hart-Davis, 1949. Ruskin's fits of insanity had already begun when he started *Praeterita*, and it was never finished.

RYDER, Dudley (Sir), 1691–1754 (p. 83). Distinguished lawyer, who became successively Solicitor-General, Attorney-General and Master of the Rolls, was knighted in 1740 and died on the day that the King signed a warrant ennobling him as Baron Ryder of Harrowby. He kept a shorthand diary while he was a student of the Middle Temple, during the years 1715 and 1716. This was transcribed and edited with an introduction by William Matthews, and published by Methuen in 1939.

SHELLEY, P. B., 1792–1822 (p. 196). Poet and Romantic rebel. Though he left no autobiography, he frequently figures in his own poems.

SOMERVILLE, Alexander, 1811–1885 (p. 40). Radical journalist. The eleventh child of an agricultural labourer in the East Lowlands, he became a trooper in the Scots Greys. His account of the appalling flogging which he received, ostensibly for insubordination but actually for sending a seditious letter to the press, is the most remarkable episode in his striking book, *The Autobiography of a Working Man,* first published in 1848, and reprinted with an introduction by John Carswell by the Turnstile Press, 1951.

SPENCER, Herbert, 1820–1903 (p. 71). Philosopher and sociologist. His massive autobiography, "a natural history of myself", was begun in 1886 when his health was failing; the bulk of it was finished by 1889, but *Reflections* were added in 1893, and the whole published the year after his death.

STEPHEN, Leslie (Sir), 1832–1904 (p. 91). Literary historian, critic and essayist. Ordained while holding an academic post at Cambridge, he relinquished holy orders because of intellectual scruples. After ten years as editor of *The Cornhill,* he became editor of the *Dictionary of National Biography.*

His autobiographical study, *Some Early Impressions*, was first published in 1903 in the *National Review*.

TOLD, Silas, 1711–1779 (p. 19). Methodist minister, who in his youth had fantastic adventures in the African slave-trade. After his conversion he worked devotedly among the condemned prisoners at Newgate, often accompanying them to Tyburn on the hangman's cart. His *Life* was first published in 1786, with a "Note to the Serious and Candid Reader" by John Wesley. It was reprinted by the Epworth Press in 1954. Vivid and ingenuous, it portrays a man of unusual spiritual gifts.

TRAHERNE, Thomas, 1637–1674 (p. 15). Priest and poet, whose *Centuries of Meditations* and *Poems* remained in manuscript till they were discovered, identified and printed by Bertram Dobell in 1908. A definitive edition appeared in 1959, edited by H. M. Margoliouth for the Oxford University Press, and a reprint of Dobell's modernised text of the *Centuries* was issued by the Faith Press, 1960.

TROLLOPE, Anthony, 1815–1882 (p. 68). Novelist. His autobiography, written in 1876, was published in 1883. A fictionalised account of how he got his clerkship in the General Post Office, referred to in this extract, can be found in *The Three Clerks*.

WALPOLE, Horace, 4th Earl of Orford, 1717–1797 (p. 86). Man of letters and connoisseur, son of the great Whig Prime Minister. Apart from *The Castle of Otranto* and his villa at Strawberry Hill, Walpole's fame rests on his brilliant letters. Various collections have appeared at intervals since his death, the standard edition being that of Mrs Paget Toynbee in 16 volumes, with supplementary volumes by Paget Toynbee (1903–1918). George Montagu, to whom this letter was addressed, had been an Eton friend, and was a rich bachelor living in the country.

WEBB, Beatrice, 1862–1948 (p. 84). Born Potter, she was the eighth daughter of a rich industrialist. She began to keep diaries at a very early age. In 1892 she married Sidney Webb, later Lord Passfield, and together they wrote extensively on issues connected with socialism. *My Apprenticeship* was first published in 1926; its sequel, *Our Partnership*, edited by B. Drake and M. I. Cole, appeared in 1950.

WELCH, Denton, 1915–1948 (p. 181). Writer of short stories and autobiographical novels. While an art student, he received serious spinal injuries in a road accident in 1943, and turned with great intensity to writing. *The Denton Welch Journals*, edited with an introduction by Jocelyn Brooke, cover the years 1942–1948; published by Hamish Hamilton, 1952.

WELLS, H. G., 1866–1946 (p. 96). Novelist and populariser of scientific notions. His frank and interesting *Experiment in Autobiography* was published by Victor Gollancz and the Cresset Press in 1934.

WESLEY, John, 1703–1791 (p. 104). Founder of Methodism, and an indefatigable keeper of journals. The standard edition of his *Journals* was issued by R. Culley, 1909–1916, edited by N. Curnock.

WHITE, J. Blanco, 1775–1841 (p. 169). Writer on religious topics. Born in Seville, he became a Roman Catholic priest, but abandoned the priesthood and the faith when he came to England in 1810. He became a Christian again, qualified as an Anglican clergyman in 1814, and later settled at Oriel College, Oxford, ending up as a Unitarian. A conspicuously honest man, there is much about his religious doubts in *The Life of Joseph Blanco White, written by himself*. This, with some of his letters, was edited by J. H. Thom, and published in 1845.

WHITEFIELD, George, 1714–1770 (p. 62). Revivalist preacher, at first an ally of the Wesleys, but later the leading light of the Countess of Huntingdon's Connection.

WORDSWORTH, William, 1770–1850 (p. 88). Poet. *Tintern Abbey* appeared in *Lyrical Ballads*, 1798.

WORTLEY MONTAGU, Lady Mary, 1689–1762 (p. 122). Letter-writer and wit. Daughter of the 5th Earl of Kingston, she eloped with Sir Edward Wortley Montagu in 1712. He went as Ambassador to Constantinople in 1716, and here her *Turkish Letters* were written. She and Pope became relentless antagonists. Her *Letters and Works* were edited by Lord Wharncliffe in 1837; enlarged and revised editions appeared in 1861 and 1893.

YEATS, W. B., 1865–1939 (p. 204). Poet, playwright, Irish Senator. This passage comes from *The Stirring of the Bones*, Book V of *Autobiographies*, published by Macmillan in 1955.

YONGE, C. M., 1823–1901 (p. 27). Prolific novelist. She was educated by her father at Otterbourne, and came under the influence of Charles Kingsley. *Charlotte Mary Yonge: her Life and Letters*, by Christabel Coleridge, 1903, incorporates some autobiographical fragments.

YOUNG, Arthur, 1741–1820 (p. 173). Secretary to the Board of Agriculture. He collected materials for a great work to be entitled "Elements and Practice of Agriculture", and wrote extensively on what he observed while travelling in England and France. His memoirs, compiled from various diaries and papers by M. Betham-Edwards, were published in 1898 as *The Autobiography of Arthur Young*.

DATE DUE

GAYLORD			PRINTED IN U.S.A.